The Square

The Story of a Saloon

RON FIMRITE

Foreword by Dan Jenkins

TAYLOR PUBLISHING COMPANY
DALLAS, TEXAS

To my wife Linda whose idea,
for better or worse,
this was in the first place.

Copyright © 1988 by Ron Fimrite

Published by
Taylor Publishing Company
1550 West Mockingbird Lane
Dallas, Texas 75235

All rights reserved.

No part of this book may
be reproduced in any form
without written permission
from the publisher.

Book design by Lurelle Cheverie

Title-page illustration
by Mary Etta Moose

Library of Congress Cataloging-in-Publication Data

Fimrite, Ron.
    The Square : the story of a saloon / Ron Fimrite ; introduction by Tom Wolfe.
      p. cm.
  ISBN: 0-87833-631-1
    1. Washington Square Bar & Grill (San Francisco, Calif.) 2. San Francisco (Calif.)—Social life and customs. I. Title.
TX950.57.C2F56 1989
647'.95794'61—dc19   88-13878
                                                                                         CIP

Printed in the United States of America
10 9 8 7 6 5 4 3 2 1

Contents

1 / If I'm Here and I Get Hungry, I'll Eat / 1

2 / A Funky Neighborhood Place / 15

3 / The Roses of Washington Square / 31

4 / A Tale of Four Cities / 39

5 / Calling Doctor Dorenbush / 51

6 / The Old Guard / 65

7 / The New Wave / 77

8 / Splendid! What's Softball? / 89

9 / Life Goes On and Then It Doesn't / 107

10 / The Flavor of North Beach / 119

11 / You're Just Selling Gin / 127

12 / Hard Times / 139

13 / We Shall Not Be Moved / 149

14 / The Future Is Now / 159

15 / Good Night, Sweetheart / 165

Epilogue / 173

Foreword

To say Ron Fimrite knows a lot about saloons is to say an Arab knows a lot about sand.
    But this is not to suggest that Ron writes most of his fetching, crystal-clear prose on napkins, in a saloon like The Square in San Francisco. The Ron Fimrite I know wouldn't be caught drunk or sober with a napkin around his glass.

Real men don't drink whiskey with napkins around their glasses.

A real man — like Ron — rattles the cubes in his empty glass as he smiles at a bartender or waiter or waitress, and this means he needs another cocktail, hold the napkin.

We have rattled a few glasses together, Ron and I — coast to coast, cab ride to cab ride, bar to bar, press box to press box. We became pals back in the days when we were on the *Sports Illustrated* campus together in Manhattan, which was a few years before I graduated from *SI* and a few years before Ron moved back to San Francisco, where it would be easier for him to pick up his mail at The Square than it was at the Ho Ho, a watering hole on 50th Street in New York that was known as a bar and *SI* hangout to some and a Chinese restaurant to others, though not to anyone who ever ate there once.

In those days, Ron and I would meet at the Ho Ho to drink whiskey and discuss the larger issues of the world, such as which editors in the Time-Life building deserved to die first, and which overrated talents among the *SI* staff writers were going to get raises ahead of us, whereupon they would have to die too.

I knew back then that Ron would someday write a terrific book about a terrific bar. It was in his genes, if it hadn't been poured down his throat.

I would like to think this book was partly inspired by "Wayne" and "Ralph," the two greatest room-clearers who ever ordered a backup.

Wayne and Ralph were born on a dark and stormy night about fifteen years ago, in the Ho Ho in Manhattan, but they have lived on to tell their tales in The Square.

Ron and I were drinking in the Chinese joint when we noticed two female researchers from *SI* taking stools at the bar. Friends and workmates.

"You girls live around here?" Ron asked them.

Suddenly, he was Wayne and I was Ralph, or I was Wayne and he was Ralph, but in any case we had our samples in the car, we had been on the road for a tough two weeks, we were having trouble getting anyone on the phone at the mill, we couldn't get delivery on our goods, and it was likely we weren't going to meet our sales quotas for the month.

It was either Wayne or Ralph who said to the bartender, "Captain, you want to spin the wheel again here?"

"Yeah, let's sprinkle the infield one more time," Wayne or Ralph replied.

"Wayne, are you still with . . . ?"

"Oh, gosh no. They cut back on my commission, so . . ."

"Same here. I went with Consolidated. Smaller area. Only six states, but . . ."

"How's the little lady?"

"Mine or yours?"

"Yours. Haven't seen her since the convention in . . . Buffalo, I guess it was."

"Oh, Jesus, did we sing some songs that night? That Sheraton hasn't been the same since."

Wayne or Ralph glanced at the bartender again. "Doctor, we need another transfusion here."

"Let me get this round, Wayne. I'm in the on-deck circle."

"I'm Ralph."

"Oh."

It didn't take all that long to clear the room.

Left alone, Ralph said to Wayne, "Gee, look at the time. Almost midnight. Better be getting home to the little lady. She likes to fix my favorite dinner when I come in off the road."

"Pigs in a blanket?"

"Creamed tuna on toast."

Over the years, Wayne and Ralph have tried hard to clear the room at The Square, but it's not possible. Either Ed Moose is interrupting or everybody's looking around for Herb Caen.

For more details, I leave it to Ron — or Wayne, or Ralph.

Dan Jenkins

KELLY. *Mr. Dowd, what is it you do?*

ELWOOD. *Harvey and I sit in the bars and we have a drink or two and play the jukebox. Soon the faces of the other people turn toward mine and smile. They are saying: "We don't know your name, Mister, but you're a lovely fellow." Harvey and I warm ourselves in all these golden moments. We have entered as strangers — soon we have friends. They come over. They sit with us. They drink with us. They talk to us. They tell about the big terrible things they have done. The big, wonderful things they will do. Their hopes, their regrets, their loves, their hates. All very large because nobody ever brings anything small into a bar. . . .*

FROM HARVEY, ACT TWO, SCENE TWO, BY MARY CHASE.

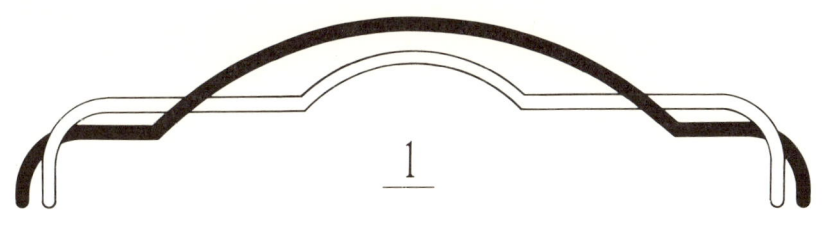

1

If I'm Here and I Get Hungry, I'll Eat

The sun fights morning clouds, strobe-lighting the poplars of Washington Square. It is the quiet time in San Francisco's North Beach, 7:00 A.M. The streets are slick and glistening from the morning mist, and they are free for the last time this day of the grumble and growl and shriek of ceaseless traffic. The bustling Chinese women who turn the sidewalks into hives have not yet emerged from their wooden houses and flats. Only the ancient Italian men in their black suits are out, wiping dry the benches of Washington Square in preparation for a long day of attending to the pigeons and exchanging sadnesses in the language of the old country.

It's a quiet time, but not in the Washington Square Bar & Grill, the little saloon across the street with the big mirrors and rust-colored walls that has been the focal point of the neighborhood for fifteen years. The Bar & Grill is known to its regulars simply as The Square, and to those who don't know any better as "The Washbag." By noon it will be throbbing with the life of the city. But even now, it is alive and kicking, an early riser.

Wally Souza, a tiny mustachioed man in his seventies, has been at his daunting labors there since 4:00 A.M. He takes out the garbage front and back. He puts the pots on the kitchen stoves. He polishes the mirrors, dusts the bar railings, empties the wastebaskets, cleans the windowsills, test flushes the toilets and turns the faucets on and off, scrubs the sinks behind the bar, wipes clean the rich French walnut wood of the bar itself, and screws in the light bulbs. Finally, he mops the marble entranceway so that it shines brightly and beams a welcome to those who cross the threshold. Wally was a butcher for forty-five years until a massive heart attack in 1976 obliged him to pursue this supposedly more sedentary line of work. He had, he says, tired of butchering, anyway. Now he loves The Square. Its people are "family."

In the kitchen, chef Richard Oku, a Polynesian who cooks Italian, presides over a teeming staff of nine. His people have been there since six, chopping and mixing and boiling. The kitchen is too small, and it is soon consumed by steam and smoke and fragrance. The white-coated cooks move as nimble phantoms through the impenetrable clouds. Through the windows of the swinging doors, the resolute Wally can be seen hurrying from chore to chore. And in the dining room, the busboys, crisp in white jackets, are setting up the thirty-one tables for lunch. It will be another hour at least before the waiters and waitresses, sleepily puffing cigarettes, arrive to change from jeans to the formal attire The Square demands of them. Time passes swiftly in these first hours.

At the stroke of nine o'clock, a stocky little man in a tweed cap and topcoat steps briskly through the back door into the steaming kitchen. He is Dennis O'Connor, one of the two day bartenders, and as he passes among the kitchen workers, he addresses them with mock formality — "Good morning, gentlemen, ladies. Good morning." He removes his coat and cap, adjusts his necktie, and heads for the bar and his "housework." Dennis looks like a cartoon Irishman, short and blocky with a broad, blue-eyed rubicund face, topped by a swatch of receding white hair. It is merely a façade. His father was indeed Irish, but his mother, far from being a daughter of the sod, was Jewish; and Dennis wears a mezuzah around his neck and a tie clasp that reads "DBLITY": Dress British, Look Irish, Think Yiddish. "I was bar mitzvahed," he says, "and then let the Jesuits educate me all the way through high school. The rabbi said I'd make a lousy Jew and the priest said I'd be a rotten Catholic. So what am I?"

The ethnic confusion befits a complicated nature. Dennis is neat to the point of fussiness, both in his dress and in his work. His shift does not actually start until ten o'clock, but he compulsively shows up an hour earlier, there to fiddle with the bottles and glasses and condiments. He stands there this morning in all of his Brooks Brothers nattiness, a stolid, affable presence. In his mid-sixties now, he looks perhaps fifty. He considers The Square a product he must sell. "If you don't have a good product, you might as well be washing cars," he says, arranging glasses. "I know the names of all the dishes we serve here. I taste the soup. I even make some suggestions on the preparation. That way I feel I can recommend things on the menu with some authority. A monkey can hand you a menu, and anybody can say, 'What d'ya want?' But you should be more than that. I don't necessarily want people to feel like they're at *home* here. I want them to feel they're out having a good time. My posture is that I'm your butler for as long as you're here."

The phone rings at nine-forty-five. It's Bobby McCambridge, the head bartender. He'll be a little late, he tells Dennis. In by ten-thirty. "Tell you what, Bobby," says Dennis. "I'll just wait here for you." He starts slicing some lemons, interrupting himself to turn the radio on to KDFC, a classical music station. Mozart echoes through the empty barroom. "I like good music. When we open, I'll switch to KJAZ (not surprisingly, a jazz station) because that's what Sam and Ed want. Fine with me. Just as long as there's no rock." Difficult as it may seem, he hums along with the Mozart.

Though his personal life has always been lived close to the edge, Dennis believes most of all in order. As the proprietor of a number of immensely popular downtown bars in the 1960s, frequently in partnership with another reckless and charming man named Gene Baskett, Dennis became something of a legend in San Francisco saloon society. His best-known joint was The Templebar, itself a local institution dating to 1907. Tucked back at the dead end of an alley off Grant Avenue in the heart of downtown, it is still in business; but chances are it will never thrive as it did nearly a quarter-century ago when O'Connor and Baskett (who died in 1981) were running it as if they were cohosts of the town's biggest cocktail party. Those were rich times in San Francisco saloon history. In the seething darkness of the old Templebar, the recorded voice of Frank Sinatra floated above hordes of well-dressed, hard-drinking young men and women. Orchestrating this nightly gavotte were Baskett, haggard and saturnine, knocking back gins with Alka-Seltzer chasers (for his ulcer); and O'Connor, elfin and unpredictable, a master at parodying his own guests. A reporter for the *San Francisco Chronicle*, assigned to do a story on singles bars during this heyday, once asked Dennis if many of the men who met women over drinks in his place rounded off the evening by dining out elsewhere. "Naw," Dennis answered, "why ruin a ten-dollar heat with a twenty-dollar dinner?" It was a response that spoke volumes on the O'Connor philosophy of life as well as on the economy of the time.

The Templebar stayed open on Saturdays, if for no other reason than to give Dennis an opportunity to clear the rubble of the Friday-night bacchanal. What few customers there were on this off day generally came in to recover lost property or to have Dennis recount for them in miserable detail events only dimly recalled from the night before. Another bartender, Jim Todt, was especially useful in this regard. Asked on a Saturday by a couple of Friday-night survivors to assess their behavior, Todt burst into a malevolent laugh and, in a voice reminiscent of Fred Allen, advised them: "Bad? You two? Why, you guys last night made the Rape of Nanking look like a sequence out of *Wee Willie Winkie*."

On one such Saturday, a rear admiral in full-dress uniform arrived at The Templebar with two attractive young women in tow. He strode confidently to the bar, elaborately ushered his companions to stools on either side of him, and then took his own seat to await service. The admiral and his ladies were the only customers there; but Dennis, normally the most attentive of barmen, scarcely glanced up at them from the sink at the opposite end of the bar, where he was scrubbing glasses with all the solemn dedication of a trusted servant polishing the family silver. The admiral could not have known, of course, that a tour of duty in the navy during World War II had left this particular Irish Jew with an abiding disrespect for authority figures. Finally, after an uncomfortable interval, Dennis lazily disengaged himself from his dishwashing chores and responded reluctantly to the repeated throat clearings and "my-good-man"s issuing from the imperious presence down the bar. He smiled pleasantly at the admiral's guests and then, when he'd achieved his station, placed both hands on the bar, leaned forward, and brusquely inquired, "What'll it be, sailor?"

Actually, it was the navy that got Dennis O'Connor to San Francisco in the first place. "We sailed under the Golden Gate and I saw this white city shining there," he says. "I fell in love right away.

I remember looking through binoculars and seeing all those wooden houses and wondering, 'Where do these people go in the winter?' I'm from Hoboken. My father was a boilermaker there. There were eight kids in the family. You know Hoboken. If they were going to give the state of New Jersey an enema, that's where they'd stick the thing."

Dennis never went back to Hoboken. His first job in San Francisco after his discharge was as a telephone repairman, work that eventually gave him a cartographer's knowledge of his adopted city. "I helped convert Chinatown from its own phone system to the telephone company's. Before we got to them, they'd just pick up a phone and an operator would answer in Chinese and they'd say, 'Give me Wong,' and she'd get Wong on the line. We improved all that. We gave them dial phones, whether they wanted them or not. No more human voices, just dial tones. Well, now these people would pick up the phone and all they'd hear was this funny buzzing noise. They were convinced their phones weren't working."

Dennis drifted gradually into his calling, the bar business. He worked first as a handyman in several spots, then as a waiter, and finally where he belonged: behind the bar. "I always knew that's what I wanted to be when I grew up." The Templebar represented the apex of his career. But he borrowed money unwisely to keep it going, fell dangerously into debt with the wrong people, and finally went bankrupt. He drove trucks after that, did public relations, worked as a house painter, moved to Phoenix and then back again to San Francisco, and married for a third time. When the job opened up at The Square, he jumped at it. He's back, he knows now, where he belongs.

Dennis looks about the same as he did twenty years ago. He has the jaunty manner and biting wit that endeared him to a generation of imbibers. But he's really a changed man. He's happily married to Linay, a bright and lively woman who is his constant companion. He's as likely now to stay home with a good book (he always was a reader) as to make the rounds. His reading serves him well behind the bar in settling customers' bets and in providing occasionally useful information, such as where Oman is on the map, what Lincoln's wife's maiden name was. Rarely now does he treat customers to his parodies of the bar types: the arrogant swinger, the lady lush, the braggart, the gay playing it straight, the hagridden spouse, the fraternity boy impressing his date. An ominous note of sincerity has crept into the old mocking manner. He will chat now at uncommon length with society matrons on a fling, reducing them to girlish giggles. And he actually seems to enjoy such high jinks. Dennis O'Connor is a happy man.

So many of his old Templebar pals now come to The Square, which is really a kindred establishment, that every day is a kind of reunion for Dennis. "Hey Dennis, remember the time . . . ?" He will remember. "In this life," he says, "you better like what you're doing or you're in trouble. That's why I'm so lucky. I love it here. Bobby does the service bar, and anybody who does that is lucky to be able to cover two stools away from the waitresses' station; so the other guy, me, has to pretty much watch the rest of the bar. There are guys in this business, you know, who just get by. They'll say, 'No fizzes today. The mixer's broke.' Suuuure. Another thing, if you don't like the job, you get picky with the customers. You end up talking to just the ones you can tolerate. Say a guy comes in wearing a baseball cap and a zipper jacket. A nerd, you say. But hey, he's still a customer. And who knows, he might own the whole city of Fremont. Yeah, he's got an American Express card, but it's platinum. The guy's heard about this place, so he decides to try it. It's your job to make him comfortable. I'll talk to that guy. Find out what he does. Chances are, I'll be interested. Hell, he'll probably turn out to be a pretty nice guy. You can't tell by the cover, can you?"

Dennis bangs the cash register. "There's an unwritten rule somewhere that a barman is going to be a thief. Maybe. You're sitting here looking at a couple thousand dollars' worth of booze and wine. There's certainly temptation. But hell, there's theft everywhere. How about the people in the office who take home all those paper clips and stamps? It's all the same thing. And the supermarket? When you look at it that way, we're not so bad, really."

It's opening time, 11:30 A.M. "When the sun hits those windshields outside," says Dennis, "I know it's eating time." Bobby McCambridge is on duty now. A man of almost laconic manner, he is the perfect complement to his relentlessly upbeat partner. At forty-five, Bobby is moon-faced and potbellied. He has a crooked smile, and he talks as if he'd been raised, as Dennis was, in New Jersey instead of Manilowoc, Wisconsin. He moved west as a teenager in 1958, "the year Lombardi got to Green Bay and the Giants moved to San Francisco." Bobby's a heavy smoker and a pretty good beer drinker. He is also, astonishingly, a distance runner who has finished ten marathons. He finished one in

New York when he was still reeling from the night before. His admirable refusal to live by the ascetic code of the marathoner has made him a favorite of feature writers and television newsmen across the country. After all, there are few stalwarts in these health-crazed days who observe Bobby's less-than-strict training regimen. So there he will be on the sports page, in all of his runner's paraphernalia, but with a cigarette dangling from his lips and a beer bottle in hand. He's a natural, a plump barfly keeping pace with the half-starved greyhounds. Well, not exactly keeping pace. Bobby has yet to break four hours in any of his marathons and he's hardly a threat to the leaders, but he does finish, and let that be a lesson for clean-livers everywhere.

"The funny thing is," says Bobby, "I took up running to lose some weight and to quit smoking and drinking. It's obvious that hasn't worked. But what the hell, I don't want to look like the rest of those guys out there, anyway."

The Square's first customer arrives by motorcycle out front. He is Scott Beach, the actor and local Renaissance man, who is just about the first customer every day. Beach has played character parts in dozens of movies, from the druggist in *American Graffiti* to the Von Braun-like rocket scientist in *The Right Stuff*, and he makes a handsome living doing voice-overs on radio and television commercials. He's also an opera singer, a poet, a songwriter, and a music critic. He is in his late fifties and paunchy, with a round, open face and a rumbling laugh. His voice is sepulchral. In the San Francisco Wax Museum's biblical section, his is the voice of God. Beach is a luncheon regular at The Square, but he is also a favored customer at Perry's on the other side of Russian Hill and at Monroe's, a small, dark, and superbly British restaurant on busy Lombard Street. He is, in fact, a star of cafe society and is much in demand at banquets and private parties. He was married for many years, and he's a father. Much of San Francisco was startled in December 1978 when, in the aftermath of the assassinations of Mayor George Moscone and Supervisor Harvey Milk, Beach announced that he was, like Milk, a homosexual. Milk's death had served to unite the city's gay community in protest, and Beach felt compelled to join many other homosexuals professing the straight life in "coming out of the closet." But the majority of his friends are still straight, and Beach has long mocked his own decision to go public with his sexual preference. "I wish I'd stayed in that closet and hired a decorator instead," he will say on the slightest provocation. Beach is not the sort to hang out in gay bars. The Square is where he's most comfortable.

Dennis pours him a Bloody Mary from the blender, a "shaker Mary," in Square parlance. Another man, well-dressed and from an old San Francisco family, plops down on the next stool and orders a Scotch on the rocks. "Bobby," he says to McCambridge, "if I leave here and somebody asks for me, I haven't been here. OK?" "Right," says McCambridge, fully comprehending. Dennis answers the phone. He is all smiles and "Yessir"s, the soul of accommodation. "Guy wants a reservation, and he wants to be sure it's in 'the main dining room.' " "The *main* dining room," he says, turning to the regulars. "In this place? He must be from L.A. Or maybe it's some office party. You know, all daiquiris and margaritas. Hooo boy. And now they tell me Senator Gore's coming in tonight with a large party." He is an Irish mother now, all wounded dignity, much put-upon, a martyr. "I swear, we day people are the last to know." With exaggerated huffiness, he serves a martini to a lawyer friend who warns him he has time for "just one, because I'm off to Baja with the girlfriend." "Oh goody," says Dennis. "And don't forget to bring your sunscreen. You're a *goy*, you know."

It is noon, Dick Partee time. Partee is a tall, tweedily dressed black man with silver hair and a round agreeable face. He is in his mid-fifties, a former "broadcast traffic manager" for the Foote, Cone & Belding advertising agency. He is also a jazz tenor sax man who began playing in the Beat jazz clubs of North Beach soon after he got out of the navy in 1953. He was among the pioneers in the poetry and jazz movement that started then, and he led the sleepless, wandering life of the itinerant jazzman, playing whenever and wherever he could get a gig, but mostly on "the Beach." Partee finally got his fill of this exhausting life by 1960, when the Beat movement itself had begun to wane. He moved to Potrero Hill, another, but somewhat more subdued, bohemian neighborhood. He has lived there ever since, the last twenty-five years with Judy Hughes, an energetic blond advertising woman who shares Partee's interest in jazz, dogs, and good books. Partee still plays regularly, with his own groups and others, occasionally at The Square itself. He has been having lunch at The Square almost daily since the place opened. "But food's not the reason I come here," he says. "It's just that this is a saloon, and if I'm here and I get hungry, I'll eat."

Partee is joined within minutes by his usual companion at the end of the bar, food critic Alan Goldman. Goldman came to San Francisco from his native New York in 1976. He was introduced to The Square by a writer friend who tired of his complaints that he couldn't find a New York-type bar in the city. "The minute I walked in here I knew I was home," says Goldman. "These were my people. I've been here ever since."

Goldman and Partee are soon involved in the conversation of the day at Bobby's end of the bar. It seems that Michael McCourt, the star bartender at Perry's, had gotten himself suspended for thirty days because, possibly in his cups, he chose to argue too vehemently with a customer. "Ah, Mike's Irish," says McCambridge. "And he had a little heat on. You know the Harps when they're sauced. Can't control themselves. And I say this from experience because I'm a Harp myself."

"Maybe so," says Partee, "but hell, he *made* Perry's. Some people just don't understand about bartenders in this town. We love 'em. You remember when Maxwell's Plum opened. Terrible place. Well, the owner told his bartenders not to invite their friends in. Didn't want them spending all their time talking to their buddies and girlfriends. That shows what that guy knows about bartenders in this town. San Franciscans go to a place just *because* they know the bartenders. We follow them around from place to place. They're stars. When you get one everyone likes, like Mike, you better treat him right. Lord knows, there are enough total assholes around. They shouldn't've let Mike go like that." Mike, as it turns out, didn't go very far; before the week was out, he was pulling shifts at The Square. And before the year was out, he was back behind the plank at Perry's.

Dennis is advising Beach of alternative ways of ordering from a bartender. "Guy comes in here the other day and I ask him, 'What'll you have?' Without cracking a smile, he says, 'I'd like a six-foot whore.'" Beach roars appreciatively. "Sounds like my father. He always said his idea of heaven was a tit filled with Scotch." The day has started.

Upstairs, in offices the size of a broom closet, Ed Moose has called a staff meeting. Ed and Sam Deitsch bought The Square together in 1973, along with Frank and Donato Rossi, owners of Gino & Carlo's, a bar a few blocks away on Green Street. The Rossis dropped out within five years, and Ed and Sam have since sold minority partnerships in the place to Mark Schachern, the bar's general manager, and to Jack Brown, a retired office-furniture company owner and Square regular. But there's no question who the boss is around there. It's Moose. He's the guy out front, the canny public-relations artist who keeps the place in the public prints. He's the political wheeler-dealer, the friend of the rich and famous, the Toots Shor, the Sherman Billingsley, the Prince Romanoff of North Beach.

Ed Moose is as big as his name. He's tall and broad-shouldered, with long limbs and enormous feet. But he's a careful dresser whose sartorial trademark is a brace of red suspenders. Sam has his own uniform: red ascot, blue work shirt, safari jacket, jeans, and white tennis shoes. Mark is the conventional dresser of the three active owners and the only one with a normal temperament. He's a cheerful man, but a worrier. Ed's wife, Mary Etta, also present, is a shy woman with a keen intelligence and a shrill laugh that will crack plaster. Before she dieted and lost fifty pounds or more, she was most often seen in smocks and muumuus. Slimmed down, she has become something of a fashion plate. Jack Brown, the silent partner, skips the staff meetings, but chef Oku is always there. The restaurant's offices are in an irreparable clutter, with sheaves of papers toppling from desks. The ceilings are so uncommonly low that Ed is barely able to stand upright and Sam, who is maybe five-foot-seven, has to duck to get through the doorway. A sign on the wall cautions all who enter, "Your Mother Doesn't Work Here. Please Pick Up After Yourself." It goes unheeded.

The meeting opens on a sour note: the crab cakes aren't moving. "It may be that they're not . . . festive enough," Mary Etta suggests. "I don't know, they go like crazy at lunch," says Ed. "What's wrong at dinner? Maybe the price. Thirteen-ninety-five might be too steep." Mumbling agreement all around. The continental breakfast, it seems, isn't doing much better than the crab cakes. "We gotta lower the price to $5.95," says Ed, suddenly the consumer's advocate. "Let's get a better muffin and see how it goes. No, that's not it. Let's give them one croissant and drop the price to $4.95. The alternative is to drop the damn thing altogether." Ed is offended by the smoked salmon. "The onion shouldn't be on top. We don't want to be telling people how their salmon should be flavored. The onion should be on the side." On to matters of greater consequence. "We got a party coming in later this week. Man named Tishman. He built the biggest housing project in the city. Seventy-five people coming. They'll take over the whole dining room. We've got to do this right. They'll want the best we can give them in wine and food."

Ed rummages through some papers on his desk. He is warily approaching a cosmic issue. "I had lunch yesterday at my favorite club, the Pacific Union Club." This elicits much chuckling. The "P.U." is the most exclusive club in town. Millionaires have died of old age just waiting to get on the membership wait-list. Only old money is any good there. When Harry Truman last visited the city, he stayed at the Fairmont Hotel across the street from the P.U. and took his morning constitutionals on Nob Hill. On one of these early walks, Truman remarked to reporters as his entourage passed by the P.U., "They pull the shades in that place when I walk by." Ed Moose will never get into the P.U. Club. But, as he has everywhere else, he has friends there. "I'm a regular," he says at The Square meeting. "I go there every ten years. So here I am having lunch there yesterday with some of the most successful people in this city, and do you know what they were talking about, these successful people? They were talking about their diets. Their damned diets!" Dieting, it goes without saying, is not a favorite topic among restaurateurs.

"It seems they got this new thing now that says your cholesterol level shouldn't be over 180 or something," Ed says, frowning. "Jesus, it used to be 300, didn't it?" "How about booze?" Sam asks hopefully. Ed rolls his eyes toward the low ceiling. "God, there was no one at the bar. Now, I ask you, what's going on around here? Used to be these people would go in and knock back their martinis and then put away a big lunch. Now all they care about is their cholesterol count. Thank God for the Olympic Club and the Bohemian where there are still some old-fashioned San Francisco boozers around. But here I am yesterday with these rich guys, these pillars of the community, all of them in the prime of life, and they're drinking bottled water and eating these little salads. It's different, I tell you. Different. What are we going to do with these people? We've gotta come up with items on our menus that will fit into their frigging diets. We can't lose lunch altogether. Jesus!"

It is a sobering thought, and they take it with them to their own lunches. At the bottom of the stairs, Ed can see Partee, Goldman, and Beach on their stools. Ed makes for the bar. "Bobby," he says, "give me a martini."

"You know what I like about this place?"

"No."

"You can talk here. You can talk about serious things. You can talk about music. About plays. About books. About writers. For days now, I've been trying to think of this writer's name. Guy used to write for The New Yorker. Wrote about people on the streets. Not the usual New Yorker stuff about professors' wives and life in the Bengal. No, this guy wrote about the real thing. About people. And he used the language of the streets. I've been trying for the life of me to think of his name. Wrote back in the forties, maybe even the thirties. Know who I mean?"

"John McNulty?"

"That's the guy. Now I ask you, how many places can you sit around the way we are and have a nice long talk about . . ."

"John McNulty."

"Right. Know what I mean?"

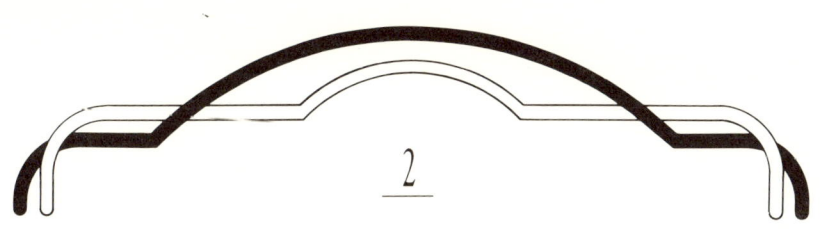

A Funky Neighborhood Place

Herb Caen, the celebrated *San Francisco Chronicle* columnist whose power is such that he can make or break a bar or restaurant with a passing mention, has called The Square "a funky neighborhood place populated by a few broken-down politicos, over-the-hill columnists, hack writers, and jazz pianists. . . . It isn't the Ritz, fergawdsakes. . . ." But Caen, who first popularized the dread "Washbag" appellation, loves the place, and even now, in his early seventies, he still plays an inning or two for The Square's peripatetic softball team. The "funky" item was written in response to some postelection remarks made in December 1987 by the then mayor-elect of San Francisco, Art Agnos. In defeating Board of Supervisors President John Molinari in a runoff election that month, Agnos had appeared before the voters as an anti-establishment man-of-the-people who would sweep out the city's Old Guard, a company that included both Mayor Dianne Feinstein and Molinari. And since Feinstein and Molinari frequented The Square, it came to represent for Agnos a bastion of Old Guardism. So obsessed was he with the notion of The Square as a seat of power and privilege that for a time it appeared he was running not so much against a county supervisor as he was against a saloon. He was further agitated knowing that both customer Caen and proprietor Moose were Molinari supporters. Caen, in fact, had written that

Molinari seemed a truer San Franciscan than the New England-reared Agnos because he was not above hanging out in joints like The Square and playing dice with the boys at the bar. Agnos, he sneered, scarcely knew where the real hangouts were.

"I'm just a middle-class person," countered Agnos in an interview with the *San Francisco Examiner*, a paper, unlike Caen's, that endorsed him. "I do middle-class things. . . . It's not just the immigrants, it's white yuppies. They come up to me and say they're glad I don't go to the Washington Square Bar & Grill. . . . I don't need to go to a place like that to know I have power. I know what my power is. I don't need to go shake dice." These aggressively humble remarks drew fire not only from Caen but from Bill Mandel, a columnist for the *Examiner*.

> It's not exactly the "funky neighborhood place" Caen calls it, since you can't expect to look into a funky neighborhood place and see the likes of Mike Royko, Jimmy Breslin, Andy Rooney, Tom Brokaw, Willie McCovey, Mario Cuomo, etc., etc., etc. On the other hand, there's nothing at all pretentious or power-spotty about the Washbag. Proprietors Ed and Mary Etta Moose, Sam Deitsch, and Mark Schachern aim to run a friendly place distinguished by good food and good drink in a relaxed atmosphere of good fellowship. They've succeeded as well or better than anyone else in San Francisco's ruthless restaurant business, which is why people with power, who could go anywhere, go to the Washbag. Famous people get treated courteously there, but so do tourists and suburbanites in for their first visit. If strangers are intimidated by the Washbag's reputation, it's not the restaurant's fault. Nothing is done to make "nobodies" feel like nobodies. Unlike many other famous places here and elsewhere, the staff is equally courteous and gracious to regulars and newcomers. Art Agnos, therefore, need not request a table in the kitchen. Even mayors are treated with respect at the Washbag.

The underlying irony in this only-in-San Francisco controversy is that all during Agnos's proletarian campaign, his top advisors, the men and women who helped create his Jacksonian image, regularly plotted their strategy over wine and pasta at . . . the Washington Square Bar & Grill.

Actually, The Square *is* a funky neighborhood saloon. It is also, albeit unpretentiously, a seat of power. And it is much more. It is a jazz club, for there is good music every night. It is, at times, an art gallery, particularly now that Mary Etta Moose has taken up painting with such enthusiasm. Artist Sam Provenzano, a Square regular who teaches both Mary Etta and Ernie McCormick, another Square regular, in his studio south of Market Street, has had several shows on the premises. Waiter Gary Epting, a successful painter on his own, uses The Square as a source of inspiration much as a somewhat better known artist once used Paris's Moulin Rouge. At his one-man show there in the winter of 1987, Epting showed portraits of nearly all the staffers and regulars. One large oil painting of a scene at the Family Table included such familiar faces as Partee, Goldman, and Jackie (Mrs. Gary) Damveld, plus the markedly unfamiliar figure of Godzilla. Critics probing for some hidden message in this peculiar work, some underlying symbolism (Moose as monster?), were quickly disabused by the artist. This was realism, pure and simple, said Epting. Godzilla (someone, that is, dressed in a Godzilla costume) did, in fact, dine at the Family Table. "It was just another one of those days when you expect almost anyone to walk in," said Epting, "and, sure enough, here comes this guy working on a movie promotion who needs a drink. He drank this gin and tonic through a hole in his chest, and seemed quite happy."

The Square is also a sports bar. Among the paintings and posters on the wall may be found memorabilia from the exploits of the bar's famous softball team. And two green chairs from the old Briggs Stadium in Detroit occupy an honored place just inside the front door, a gift to The Square from Paul Witteman, a *Time* magazine writer who has been a bureau chief both in San Francisco and Detroit. The chairs may strike an outsider as anomalous, but, in fact, this bar is a hotbed of Tigermania. Part-owner Mark Schachern, sometime-publicist Glenn Dorenbush, waitress Arlene Boyle, and waiters Epting, Jim Gallup, and Rick Snyder are all Michigan natives. Detroit manager Sparky Anderson feels so at home among these kindred spirits that he regularly lunches at The Square when the Tigers come to town to play the Oakland Athletics. The ballpark chairs were christened with champagne in 1981 by Hank Greenberg, the Tigers' Hall of Fame star. A memorable luncheon after the ceremony lasted just long enough for Greenberg to miss his return flight to Beverly Hills. "We gotta do this again," said Greenberg on finally departing. Alas, he died before he had the chance.

The Square

Greenberg was but one of any number of celebrity luncheon guests Moose habitually invites to join staffers and select customers at the Family Table, an oaken artifact that when stretched to capacity with additional leaves can seat fifteen. It looks more like a butcher's block than a dining table, but the Family Table is the closest thing The Square has to a banquet room. The great bandleader Woody Herman was another guest there, and so was jazz pianist Earl "Fatha" Hines. Hines, in fact, gave his last public performance on The Square's battered Yamaha piano.

It's true The Square is a bit on the funky side. And famous persons do eat and drink there. Almost any author plugging a book will end up there sooner or later. Visiting newsmen seldom miss spending at least one long night in the place. And The Square has such a jazzy feel to it that, more or less spontaneously, such artists as Stan Getz, Al Cohn, Dave Frishberg, Lou Levy, and Shelly Manne have played there.

But famous people have not made the place what it is. Mostly, it's just a good saloon. "It's noisy in here," a newcomer once remarked, "but it's a good noise."

"What I like about it is that it's a stand-up saloon," says Square bartender Neil Riofski. "The place has a reality to it. It's an adult room, no goofy kids. It's not a body shop, a meat market. Women feel comfortable in here because nobody's gonna hustle them. It's a place where you feel part of the crowd, even if you're a stranger."

"Very lively people come in here," says Mary Etta Moose. "They give off an energy we all draw from. There is a symbiosis quickly established. It's marvelous to watch total strangers come in here and feel that. A bar, you know, is a complex culture. Everything radiates from the bar itself. It gives light, intensity, soul to a room . . . whether people are drinking Perrier or Tanqueray."

That puts The Square firmly in the great tradition of San Francisco saloons, and, for better or worse, this is a city that for nearly one hundred fifty years has been the biggest bar town in the country. Statistics from the California Department of Alcoholic Beverage Control show that there's at least one bar for every six hundred San Franciscans. The city once actually took pride in its bibulous reputation. "Hail to the San Franciscan, whose cool climate both fosters a desire for liquor and enables him to carry it," an anonymous admirer once proclaimed. The current mood, at a time when temperance seems once again on the rise, is more one of embarrassment. The truth is that though joggers may come and go, San Francisco will probably always be a drinking man's town. In the beginning, for that matter, it was almost exclusively a man's town. Not many of the forty-niners could afford to bring their families west with them for the Gold Rush, and many were simply adventure-seeking bachelors. The saloons and the bawdy houses were their social life, and it was a life that could prove hazardous to a miner's health beyond hangovers and venereal disease.

Indeed, the saloons of the old Barbary Coast were not exactly places a fellow would choose to drop in for a quick one on the way home from the office. A cocktail served in, say, the Bull Run Concert Saloon might well be a Mickey Finn, a drink laced with knockout drops that would leave the imbiber unconscious and vulnerable to foul play. The Mickey Finn was, in many cases, merely the first step in the business of shanghaiing, a practice that originated on the San Francisco waterfront. A shanghai victim, Mickey Finned into oblivion, would then be transported from his bar stool to a ship waiting in the harbor. Upon awakening he would discover he had become a seaman obliged to labor long hours in the employ of some tyrannical Wolf Larsen type. And the ship might well have been en route to Shanghai, since San Francisco was, then as now, the gateway to the Orient.

If the Barbary Coast barhopper managed to escape being shanghaied, he was still left vulnerable to the ministrations of the "hurdy-gurdy girls" who worked in somewhat more savory saloons. San Francisco was the birthplace of the hurdy-gurdy house or "pretty-waiter saloon," as one proprietor labeled such places. Hurdy-gurdy was an offshoot of "honky-tonk," an expression used to describe saloons with girls and music. In New Orleans, where honky-tonk first thrived, some of these barroom-bordellos were quite remarkable for their elegance. So were many of their successors in San Francisco. These girlie palaces were given their generic name by the German immigrants who reached the city during the Gold Rush. The cheap piano music the bars offered reminded the Germans of the hurdy-gurdy organs played by street musicians at county fairs in the old country. The pianists in such places were invariably known as "the perfessor," and they were, in a sense, parody versions of the old German academic musicians. Some of the fancier hurdy-gurdy houses even employed violinists, one of whom, Charley Schultze, could bring tears to the eyes of the toughest customers at the Bella Union with his rendition of "Flowers on My Sainted Mother's Grave." But good music was not the staple of the hurdy-gurdy houses; bad girls were. The hurdy-gurdy girl would apparently be matching the customer drink for drink while actually downing nothing stronger than mild tea or colored sugar water. A man in the clutches of one of these femmes fatales would finish his evening drunk, broke, and invariably sexually unfulfilled. And if he hadn't spent every penny buying drinks over the bar, chances are his pocket would have been picked by his charming companion.

Hurdy-gurdy girls were of every nationality and ethnic persuasion, reflections in themselves of the melting pot San Francisco had become. A contemporary observer once remarked that "here were British subjects, Frenchmen, Germans and Dutch, Italians, Spaniards, Norwegians, Swedes and Swiss, Jews, Turks, Chinese, Kanakas, New Zealanders, Malays and Negroes, Parthians, Medes and Elamites, Cretes and Arabians, and the dwellers in Mesopotamia and Cappadocia, in Boston and New Orleans, Chicago and Peoria, Hoboken and Hackensack." Even that was an incomplete roll call. Missing from it were the Indians and Mexicans who were native to the state, as well as the Chilean women who made up the majority of the town's prostitutes. Indeed, there was something for everyone in the hurdy-gurdy bars. The Aguila de Oro offered a "chorus of Ethiopians"; the Bella Union, Mexican Fandango dancers; the Alhambra, a cancan line. And the advertisements for these places were admirably straightforward:

AT THE BELLA UNION
you will find
PLAIN TALK AND BEAUTIFUL GIRLS!
REALLY GIRLIE GIRLS!
No back numbers, but as Sweet and Charming Creatures as
ever Escaped a Female Seminary.
Lovely Tresses!! Lovely Lips! Buxom Forms!
at the
BELLA UNION

Some of the advertising appeared in the guise of legitimate news stories. A correspondent from the *San Francisco Call* once included in his supposed diatribe against the Barbary Coast the names and addresses of some of the more disreputable establishments. Then he advised the reader, "We give the precise locality so our readers may keep *away*." Another report of the time might well have aroused the curiosity of the more adventurous readers: "The Barbary Coast is the haunt of the low and the vile of every kind. . . . Licentiousness, debauchery, misery, poverty, wealth, profanity, blasphemy, and death are there. And Hell, yawning to receive the putrid mass, is there also." Sounds like a lively crowd.

Those years provided an undeniably colorful if not entirely savory chapter in the city's history, and were, for that matter, important ones in the history of bar culture in America. Gold dust was the original currency of the Barbary Coast. A shot of whiskey could be purchased for a pinch of dust held between thumb and forefinger. Thus the expression "In a pinch." The martini, San Francisco historians insist, was invented in a local bar. The common view is, of course, that the drink got its name from the Martini & Rossi Company, makers of its secondary ingredient, vermouth. Not so, say Bay Area experts, among them the late historian of slang, Peter Tamony. The drink was conceived and first poured by the legendary Barbary Coast bartender Jeremy Thomas in the El Dorado saloon as a bracer for customers taking the ferry from San Francisco to Martinez across the bay. It was first known as the Martinez Cocktail, then simply the Martinez, and, finally, the Martini. Thomas, the first in a distinguished line of famous San Francisco barmen, could not have known at the time that he had created a monster. A contemporary rival, Duncan Nichol, invented a drink, the Pisco Punch, which in nineteenth-century San Francisco was every bit as popular as Thomas's martini. The principal ingredient was Peruvian Pisco brandy, but Nichol took the rest of the recipe to the grave with him. Obviously, it was quite a drink. Richard Erdoes, in his excellent history *Saloons of the Old West*, describes the reaction of one imbiber to his first Pisco Punch:

> It is perfectly colorless, quite fragrant, very seductive, terribly strong, and has a flavor somewhat resembling that of Scotch whiskey, but much more delicate, with a marked fruity taste. . . . We had some hot, with a bit of lemon and a dash of nutmeg in it. . . . The first glass satisfied me that San Francisco was, and is, a nice place to visit. . . . The second glass was sufficient, and I felt that I could face smallpox, all the fevers known to the faculty, and the Asiatic cholera combined, if need be.

The Button Punch was a direct descendant of the Pisco Punch, also with Peruvian brandy as a base, and, according to Erdoes, it moved none other than Rudyard Kipling to rapture. The Button Punch, wrote Kipling, "is the highest and noblest product of the age. . . . I have a theory it is compounded of cherubs' wings, the glory of a tropical dawn, the red clouds of sunset, and fragments of lost epics by dead masters."

Erdoes tells us that the Oyster Cocktail was also invented in San Francisco, at Moraghan's Oyster Palace by a customer who inadvertently dropped one of the house delicacies in his whiskey and decided on impulse to down the whole thing. He was so pleased with the result that he repeated the procedure, again and again. Some say Chop Suey was similarly conceived in a San Francisco bar. A harried Chinese chef, running behind in his orders, simply dumped everything left in the kitchen in a large bowl and called it "Chop Sui," which is Chinese for odds and ends. The dish was an instant success with everyone but the Chinese, who knew better.

In time the Barbary Coast saloons took on a veneer of civilization. Lola Montez, a Spanish dancer and mistress of such nineteenth-century luminaries as Dumas Père and Franz Liszt, performed her famous Spider Dance at the old Bella Union. Dolores McCord, also a Dumas sweetheart who performed under the name of Adah Isaacs Menken, acted Lord Byron's *Mazeppa* at Maguire's Theater Saloon, stunning the audience to sobriety with a finale that had her being packed off to her doom by a wild horse. And Sarah Bernhardt made San Francisco a stop on one of her numberless retirement tours. But homegrown girls had the bigger reputations. One such, a madam named Tessie Wall, was famous for being able to drink any man in town under the table. It was said, in fact, that Tessie once tossed back twenty-two bottles of French champagne at a single sitting.

An 1892 state law that prohibited the serving of liquor during a theatrical performance brought some order to the usual chaos and hastened the closing of many of the bawdier hurdy-gurdy houses. By the turn of the century, San Francisco had assumed its proper place as the financial, political, and cultural capital of the Far West. At the same time, it had developed a rigid social structure topped off by the nabobs of Nob Hill. But it never did shake off its reputation as a haven for the drinking man. Not even the 1906 earthquake and fire could curb the city's powerful thirst. And from the rubble of that formidable disaster, newer and even fancier saloons sprang forth.

Prohibition spawned an impressive array of back-alley speakeasies, the most celebrated of which was Izzy Gomez's shabby little hideaway at 848 Pacific Avenue. Gomez operated from a garage-top loft that was reached by way of a rickety staircase. The proprietor was a portly man with sleepy eyes and a snub nose with flared nostrils. He had a drooping mustache that at least partially deflected his cigarette ashes from the drinks he served. Gomez wore baggy black suits, an incongruous gold watch chain and a wide-brimmed fedora that was never, under any circumstances, removed. He reigned over his tiny domain from a perch atop a bar stool in back of the bar, dispensing inimitable wisdom to a clientele largely composed of writers and artists. Gomez's place remained popular through the thirties, and it was immortalized by one of his regular customers, William Saroyan, as "Nick's" in the Pulitzer Prize-winning play *The Time of Your Life*.

Shanty Malone, a black-haired Irishman from the Pacific Northwest, was another legendary saloonkeeper who stayed one step ahead of the law. In Shanty's case, almost literally, one step. Every time he was raided during Prohibition, Shanty moved to a different location. His frequent comings and goings in no way discouraged his loyal army of regulars, who always managed to find the newest Shanty's. Unlike Gomez, Shanty catered to a sporting crowd, and it was not unusual after a Saturday football game to see players and coaches of the competing teams replaying the contest on Shanty's sawdust floor. Repeal scarcely eased Shanty's troubles with the police, for it was his view that the 2:00 A.M. closing time imposed by state law was grossly unfair to his customers, most of whom were just hitting their stride at that hour. Besides, at two in the morning Shanty himself had joined the party. So, though drinking was now legal, Shanty kept on the move. In one of his last places, on Sansome Street across from the Federal Reserve Bank, the windows fronting the street were painted a dark and impenetrable green, not so much to proclaim the proprietor's Gaelic heritage as to discourage the prying eyes of the law. A customer arriving after the legal closing hour had only to rap on the door, call out Shanty's name, and properly identify himself to gain entry into a swarming crowd of newspapermen, college kids, old vaudevillians, and aging sports heros.

The interior was dank and unappealing. Yellow photographs hung disjointedly on the walls; somebody was usually playing the piano and an Irish tenor would be singing. The floor was thick with sawdust, broken glass, and unidentifiable debris. One morning, after Shanty had ushered the last party goer out into the sunlight, an eager young cleanup man began attacking the rubble on the floor with a broom. "Stop! For Christ's sake, stop," Shanty cried out, right hand clutching his heart. "You're sweeping out the atmosphere."

Cookie Picetti opened his Star Buffet on Kearny Street across from the old Hall of Justice in the mid-1930s. Like Shanty's and Izzy's before it, Cookie's was a mess, a calculatedly dark and gloomy cavern flanked usually by a laundry and a Chinese restaurant. Cookie's was patronized mostly by denizens of the nearby Hall, cops and defendants, mouthpieces and prosecutors, bail bondsmen and jailors, all fueled to bonhomie by the crusty barkeep's minuscule doses of whiskey and gin. Anything more complicated than bourbon or Scotch on the rocks was frowned upon by the single bartender on duty, Cookie himself. Cookie's customers were so loyal that they still found their way back to the Kearny Street hole long after the old Hall of Justice was shut down and a new one opened on the other side of town, near a Bay Bridge on-ramp. And Cookie served them up to his eightieth birthday. He might have served them longer, for that matter, had he not suffered a broken hip in a nasty fall outside the joint.

At Coffee Dan's, which flourished in the thirties and forties, customers were given tiny hammers with which to express their reactions to the entertainment, usually provided by the customers themselves. There was very little shouting in Coffee Dan's, but on a busy night the place sounded like a construction project. LaRocca's corner featured Friday-night concerts performed by Leo LaRocca himself and his two sons, Vince and Jack. An otherwise unremarkable, even folksy place, LaRocca's was transformed into a den of mystery and glamour one morning in 1947 when the bullet-riddled body of a notorious mafioso, Nick deJohn, was found in the trunk of a car parked outside the bar. At the Bocce Ball, also in North Beach, patrons were encouraged to sing, and since many of them were unemployed opera or light opera performers, the quality of entertainment was many degrees higher than that of, say, Coffee Dan's. There was opera, too, and there still is, at Tosca on Columbus Avenue, but you will find it there on the jukebox. Much of North Beach now jangles to the sound of rock, but in the neighborhood's glory years, Caruso's was the dominant voice.

The newspaper crowd has always had its sanctuaries. Breen's, boasting the longest (seventy-two feet) bar in the land, serviced the *Examiner*, when it was at Third and Market streets, as did Jerry and Johnny's; and Hanno's, now in its third location, still accommodates the *Chronicle*, along with the M&M. *Chronicle* columnist Stanton Delaplane made the Buena Vista Cafe perhaps the city's best-patronized bar in the fifties and sixties when he wrote about a drink he introduced there, Irish Coffee. Within a year of Delaplane's first column on the drink, the "B.V." was pouring more "Irishes" than were served in all of Ireland.

An entirely different sort of bar began to make its appearance in San Francisco in the late 1950s and early 1960s. North Beach had been a refuge for bohemians from the city's earliest history, and there were bars catering to this element on virtually every street corner, but, with one notable exception, they were little known outside the neighborhood. The Black Cat, drawing inspiration, presumably, from the famous Parisian Left Bank cabaret of the *fin de siècle*, was that exception. Proclaiming itself "the seacoast of bohemia," the Cat reached its pinnacle in the years immediately following Repeal. By the late 1930s it had achieved a national reputation as the sort of dive one might expect to find in the Berlin of Christopher Isherwood. Its clientele, in all of its eccentric variety, was depicted in a 1938 painting by California artist Ralph Sampson that hung on the wall opposite the bar. The Cat was so notorious by World War II that it was declared off-limits to all military personnel. It enjoyed a brief revival after the war, but its bohemian patrons had mostly moved on. By the late forties, it had become a predominantly gay bar, frequented, particularly on weekends, by transvestites. In 1963, it closed forever.

The forerunner of the new bohemian bar was the Vesuvio Cafe, which opened in a dilapidated Victorian building at the corner of Adler Alley and Columbus Avenue in 1949. Its proprietor was Henri Lenoir, a jaunty North Beach character of long standing, familiar even to strangers outside the neighborhood as the little man in the big beret. The Vesuvio became an almost instant hangout of the artistic set, who, with Tosca and Twelve Adler across the street, now had an established circuit to follow. And then in June 1953, the City Lights bookstore was opened just across the alley from the Vesuvio by a young poet and World

War II veteran named Lawrence Ferlinghetti, and an English instructor from San Francisco State College (now University), Peter Martin. Martin had the added distinction of being the son of Carlo Tresca, an Italian anarchist who was assassinated ten years earlier. But Martin was gone within a year, and the bookstore soon became an extension of Ferlinghetti's vibrant personality (though he eventually took in a new partner, Shigeyoshi Murao). The store published its own radical and avant-garde literary magazine, *City Lights*, and in 1955 began publishing books, one of which would become the manifesto of a generation. *Howl and Other Poems* by Allen Ginsberg appeared under the City Lights emblem in 1956. Upon publication of *Howl*, Ferlinghetti was arrested for selling obscene literature, and his trial became a national bohemian *cause célèbre*. The court ruled that *Howl* and its publisher were protected by the First and Fourteenth Amendments and that the book was not obscene because it was of "redeeming social importance." *Howl* would be the first salvo fired by the new bohemians, a group soon to be known as The Beat Generation.

The Beats — or "Beatniks," as Caen, drawing from the Sputnik experience, preferred to call them — were bar people. Many of those, in the first wave at least, were war veterans, so they were not just kids, as were their successors, the Hippies. They liked hanging out together in congenial surroundings, preferably with jazz playing in the background, at places where they could share their passionate distaste for the bourgeoisie over bottles of cheap domestic red wine. New bars all over North Beach began springing forth to accommodate them. The Coffee Gallery, on the site of a former lesbian bar named Miss Smith's Tea Room, featured poetry readings and the comedy monologues of the British hipster, Lord Buckley. The Place on upper Grant Avenue had a weekly Blabbermouth Night, during which customers were encouraged (not that they required encouragement) to hold forth on any subject that agitated them, that usually being the evils of squaredom. The Anxious Asp posted a warning on its front door: "Crapulous Eleemosynaries Keep Out." The Co-Existence Bagel Shop became the unofficial headquarters of the movement and, in time, a fortress against police raiders. The Cellar on Green Street, just off Grant, held poetry and jazz nights, in which poets would recite to jazz accompaniment. Kenneth Rexroth, poet, author, journalist, and by then middle-aged radical, was the star of these innovative sessions. His *Thou Shalt Not*

Kill, an ode to Dylan Thomas, had in it the rallying cry of the movement: "You killed him, you son of a bitch in your Brooks Brothers suit. . . ." Rexroth was, like so many of the early Beats, a serious artist. Others prominent at the time were Ferlinghetti and Ginsberg of course, and Jack Kerouac, Gregory Corso, Gary Snyder, Kenneth Patchen, Michael McClure, and Richard Brautigan; along with such peripheral figures as Neal Cassady, the inspiration for Kerouac's novel *On the Road* (which became the Beat Bible), and Bob Kaufman, a half-black-half-Jewish poet and rebel who became, for the police, Public Beatnik Number One. Kaufman was locally famous as a symbol of Beat disaffection, but in Europe he was considered a major poet, "the black-American Rimbaud."

Unfortunately, not all of the Beats were artists. As time passed, there were more poseurs than poets in North Beach, and instead of shunning the square world outside, as the first Beats had, the newcomers seemed determined to put on a show for the ever-increasing crowds of tourists who were drawn to the neighborhood by overwhelming publicity. One so-called Beat notoriously dressed himself in the costume of a sixteenth-century cavalier. What had begun as a serious literary rebellion had devolved into a freak show. North Beach was now attracting runaway teenagers, drug addicts, and fugitives from the law, all posing as Beats. The movement could not carry the weight of this unwanted influx and, within a decade, it collapsed in a tawdry heap. And the remarkable little bars it had spawned began, one by one, to shut down until only The Coffee Gallery was left. And when it closed its doors in 1980, a sorry anachronism, they were all gone without a trace.

A young man and woman, both in their twenties, are ushered to a table near the piano. Mike Lipskin, the master of the stride idiom, is playing a medley of Fats Waller pieces. The young couple nods in appreciation. This could well be a first date, for the two seem ill at ease, unsure of the next step. They try conversation over the insistent pounding of the piano.

SHE. I just love jazz, don't you? It's so much more . . . well, classical than rock, don't you think?

HE. Oh yeah, much more. Hey, what would you like to hear? Maybe I can get this guy to play something for us.

SHE. Well . . .

HE. C'mon, I'm sure he can play anything. That's what he's here for.

SHE. Actually, I do have a favorite. I think what's his name . . . Lou Armstrong . . . used to play it. . . .

HE. Just give me the title. I'll get this guy to play it.

SHE. Oh, it's right on the tip of my tongue. . . .

HE. Yeah?

SHE. I've got it! Ask him if he knows, "When the Shark Bites."

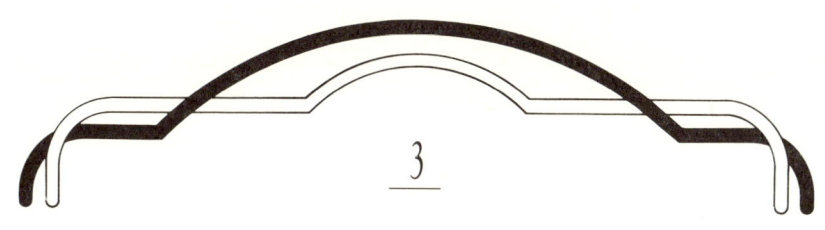

3

The Roses of Washington Square

T he Square is not by any definition, certainly not bartender Riofski's, a body shop or a meat market. That is to say a young buck on the prowl would do much better plying the discos of SOMA (South of Market Street) or the teeming lounges of the so-called Bermuda Triangle at the corner of Fillmore and Greenwich streets, where attractive young women habitually disappear from bar stools at any of the three yuppie bars there. It's not that romance doesn't flourish at The Square or that it is strictly a male bastion. Oh, my yes, there is romance there. The purplish walls fairly throb with it. It's just that the pace of it, in keeping with the generally mature years of the established regulars, is more measured. Love at The Square is slower and sadder, an autumn leaf, not a spring flower.

Women, singly or in groups, stride regularly up to the bar, bid a cheery hello to Dennis or Bobby or Neil or Al or Bob, and confidently order their drinks. "It's a great place for us," says Blanche Streeter, doyenne of The Square's corps of single working women. "If somebody offers you a drink, the bartender will always ask you first if you want to accept. At most bars, they'll just send the drink over and leave you on your own. The Square is very good at keeping the louts at bay."

Ed and Sam, the resident social arbiters, have no set policy in this regard, as Jack Koeppler did at the old Buena Vista Cafe in its salad days a generation ago. At a time, the presexual revolution, when the respectable pickup or "action" bars were just beginning to catch fire (Dennis O'Connor's Templebar was the class of the genre), Koeppler laid down a draconian edict: any male caught attempting to buy a drink for an unattached female customer was to be automatically ejected. Moose, with his strict Catholic schooling, is naturally repelled by the unseemly fawning and pawing that goes on in many of The Square's sister saloons, and Sam, no prude but fastidious by nature, regards such juvenile byplay as unworthy of a joint so avowedly hip. And formidable women of the Streeter stripe have no difficulty keeping the overtly amorous at arm's length. So to the naked eye The Square may seem as sexless as a mausoleum. Ah, but beneath that pallid surface, the place smolders. It can be as steamy there as in the most decadent Berlin cabaret or Left Bank bistro.

Blanche Streeter usually knows where the bodies are buried. At first glance, this attractive dark-haired woman seems the embodiment of sophistication. But Blanche was as callow as a milkmaid when she first came to San Francisco from Montreal in 1957 as a twenty-year-old housewife and mother. After a divorce left her with three small children to raise, she found work in the *Chronicle's* circulation department. It was a job that paid a pittance and challenged her to do nothing more intellectually stimulating than take subscription orders on the telephone. She discovered, however, that working for a newspaper, even at such an unglamorous job, was not a bad way to meet men. And most of the interesting men, she observed, were the reporters and editors, almost all of whom seemed to adjourn after — and often during — a day's work to Hanno's Bar at the corner of Minna and Mary streets (it had moved from its original location at Fifth and Mission).

Blanche entered the newspaper business at a time in San Francisco, in the late fifties and early sixties, when it yet retained some of the screwball romance of the front-page era. There were just enough of the old Hecht–MacArthur-style reporters around to keep the tradition alive, and the younger ones emulated rather than rejected their seniors' eccentric ways. Newspaper reporters in the San Francisco of that time were as remote from the sobersided functionaries of today's computerized journals as the linotype machine is from the word processor. There was also in that riotous time a circulation war raging between the previously fat cat *Examiner* and the upwardly striving *Chronicle*. Two other papers, the *News* and the *Call Bulletin*, looked on helplessly as the big guns blazed away at each other. The war would end by treaty in 1965 when the competitors merged their business and advertising departments and carved up the circulation so that the *Chronicle*, the real winner in the war, was awarded the lucrative morning market while the *Examiner*, the front-runner for more than seventy-five years, was stuck with the dwindling afternoon business. The *Call* and the *News* first merged with each other, and then with the *Examiner*, before they finally disappeared altogether.

But when Blanche went to work for the *Chronicle*, the place was humming with excitement. Scott Newhall, an executive editor who might charitably be called eccentric, had in a few short years transformed a relatively stodgy and "responsible" journal, the self-proclaimed *New York Times* of the West, into the most bizarre daily publication in the country. Newhall considered straight news no more palatable than porridge. Instead of the conventional cops-and-robbers and city-hall stuff the *Examiner* churned out daily, Newhall chose, rather, to do an exposé on the bad coffee served in San Francisco restaurants; he called it "A Great City Forced to Drink Swill." He dispatched Bud Boyd, an otherwise nondescript fish-and-game editor, into the wilderness — "The Last Man on Earth" — to prove that a resourceful outdoorsman could survive a nuclear attack by living off the land, a premise neatly shot full of holes after an *Examiner* search team discovered Boyd's camp and found discarded cans of spaghetti and other store-bought comestibles. Newhall hired a hairdresser to write an antifeminist column, dubbed him Count Marco, and had him "cover" (with a ghost writer) a marriage-triangle murder trial in Los Angeles. He sent reporter George Draper, himself a marvelous eccentric, to Africa, ostensibly to cover the various revolutions then raging on the continent, but primarily to come up with *Chronicle*-type stories. Draper dutifully filed an interview with a pygmy chieftan who told the intrepid reporter that he had never heard of anyone named Patrice Lumumba and that, in fact, he wasn't sure where in the great forest this place called the United States of America was. Draper also covered in poker-faced prose a farcical campaign by mock moralists (actually, Hollywood actor-writer Buck Henry and professional prankster Alan Abel) to clothe naked animals. To illustrate this story, the *Chronicle* ran a front-page photo of the bogus bluenoses struggling to fit a bull elephant into a pair of enormous boxer shorts.

For these and other similarly off-the-wall japes — the *Chronicle* sponsored an Emperor Norton Treasure Hunt in San Francisco and a camel race in Virginia City, Nevada — Newhall had assembled a staff of clever writers, many of them carefree young men fresh out of Bay Area and Ivy League universities. David Braaten, one of these master farceurs, led off a story on a female shark systematically devouring her mate at the San Francisco aquarium with, "Not satisfied with half a man . . ." And when Newhall learned that the male gorilla imported specifically to mate with the San Francisco Zoo's resident female ape was steadfastly ignoring her, he dispatched an ace reporter to find out why. The ensuing story concluded that while no firm reason for the young male's airy detachment could be established, it might well be related to the fact that his cave in the gorilla grotto was decorated with Japanese prints and that he spent languid hours there absorbed in listening to Marlene Dietrich and Judy Garland recordings. Donovan McClure, a *Chronicle* reporter who later became chief of public relations for the Peace Corps, wrote of an inmate on San Quentin's Death Row who was so impatient for the inevitable that he petitioned the state to "get cracking and give him the gas." Obviously, only lively writing could rescue Newhall's implausible "news stories" from absurdity. But the *Chronicle*'s bright young men were driving more-orthodox *Examiner* newsmen bananas and finally, much to Newhall's agitation, to the peace table. What the *Chronicle* editor had in mind all along was driving them right out of business.

Every night during the cocktail hour (which, some said, ran from 9:00 A.M. to 2:00 A.M.) these *Chronicle* wits would assemble in Hanno's dingy confines to play liar's dice and recap the day's zaniness. Fascinated by this daily migration of presumably eligible males, Blanche Streeter decided to take the plunge herself. She persuaded some of her female colleagues to join her after work for drinks in the newsmen's sanctuary. Actually, Hanno's, unlike most newspaper bars of the time, was far from a stag enclave. Television station KRON had its offices then in the *Chronicle* building, and its women employees routinely went to Hanno's. So did any number of public-relations women and the various mistresses of reporters and editors. *Examiner* reporters may have spent their time at Jerry and Johnny's or Breen's trading the latest jokes or rehashing anecdotes; the *Chronicle* kids were getting laid.

Blanche found she could hold her own at Hanno's, and through the pals she made there she gained unexpected entree into the city's literary community. But Blanche, along with hundreds of other *Chronicle* and *Examiner* business employees, lost her job when the two papers merged, or, as the official euphemism had it, formed a "joint operating agreement." She also got considerable publicity of her own when she sued for compensation for the loss of her job. By the 1970s Blanche Streeter had become a rather well known San Francisco woman about town, and in 1975, Pied Piper (Glenn) Dorenbush (of whom more later) persuaded her to come by this new restaurant in North Beach he called The Square. She found it considerably more chic than the old Hanno's, but she also noticed that it seemed to attract the same sort of bright, adventurous crowd. Blanche was hooked on the place, and later, when she went to work for the Grubb & Ellis real-estate firm, she persuaded her female colleagues to join her there for regular luncheons. It was, they all agreed, a pretty good place to meet men, if that's what they wanted, and a great place just to have a good time, with or without men. Blanche also found she could entertain business clients there without enduring the messy ordeal of fighting for the check after lunch. At The Square, such lunches were merely charged without fuss to her own bill.

Blanche's original group, which included not only the real-estate women but the glamorous society aerobics instructor Martha Cason Major and the pert *Examiner* columnist Stephanie Salter, became fixtures, The Square's sorority. The women composed and sang songs on St. Patrick's Day for the Irish male bloc led by police inspector Chris Sullivan, and they entered The Square's annual Penny Pitch competition as a team, "The Roses of Washington Square." Roses such as Salter and lawyer Patsy Glynn have brought more than mere feminine wiles to this bizarre athletic event, for they have often upset boastful males on their way to the semifinals or even the finals. The real-estate sorority has also been the repository of The Square's rapidly accumulating gossip. "Look out," an unwary philanderer may be warned, "you're on the Grubb & Ellis wire service."

The Roses themselves have scarcely been immune to gossip and romance. Their resident wit and principal songwriter, Ellen Edmondson, began a long and certainly stormy affair with the ever-present Sullivan inside The Square's purplish walls. It was a romance launched by a poem Edmondson wrote in the Dorothy Parker mode; it needled the policeman for not calling her, and the affair has survived nearly a decade of noisy breakups and tearful reconciliations.

Blanche herself has entertained many a beau at The Square. And there even have been times when her hard-won independence seemed threatened by dread matrimony. She actually allowed one suitor to accompany her on The Square softball team's first road trip, to Paris in 1979. This, as we shall see later, was an excursion memorable for high jinks of every sort, but Blanche and her lover seemed well above the fray until the very last two days, when her man began disappearing at odd hours. And as the trip wound down, this once-passionate pursuer grew increasingly cool and remote. When they returned finally to San Francisco, he promptly terminated the relationship. Blanche was stunned. Then she learned why it had all ended so suddenly and so badly: her beau had fallen hard for the pretty travel agent who had accompanied the team abroad. He and the agent were, in fact, married within a year after the game and resettled in Marin County across the Golden Gate.

Blanche Streeter is not one to be troubled overlong by setbacks of this nature. She has too full and active a life, one in which every day has its quota of peril and promise. In fact, she says, "I'd say I've had adequate revenge. After all, the poor man is now a suburban house husband. That's punishment enough."

"So you're in public relations, are you?"

"Well, we're really just starting up again. It's the Sesnon-Hill agency. We were pretty big a few years back."

"Sesnon-Hill? Say, weren't you people involved in that Par Course fiasco? And Insuragram? Didn't that company go bust?"

"Yes, they did, I'm proud to say."

"Proud?"

"Yes..."

"Dennis, would you bring the young lady another screwdriver. Now, as you were saying..."

"Thanks. Yes, you see our company has what you might call a specialty."

"Most PR outfits do. What's yours?"

"We make things disappear. You wanna get lost, you come to Sesnon-Hill. I don't care how famous you are, we can get you lost in no time at all."

"I suppose Judge Crater was one of your clients."

"He certainly was. And Amelia Earhart. Glenn Miller hired us. Tom Snyder was a major client. And remember William Miller, Goldwater's running mate? One of our favorites."

"I think I get the picture...."

"And then there was Ambrose Bierce. Jimmy Hoffa, certainly. The McGuire Sisters. Tiny Tim. Walter Mondale...."

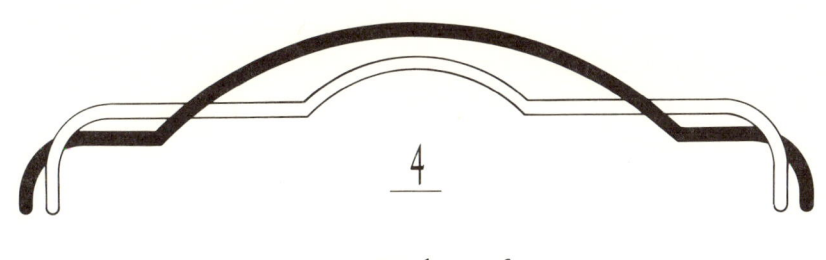

4

A Tale of Four Cities

There is nothing in his ancestry, upbringing, education, experience, or philosophy to suggest that Edward Moose IV should have been a tavern owner or, for that matter, a San Franciscan, both of which he now is heart and soul. He didn't even expect to live this long. When his Irish-Scandinavian father died of a brain tumor at age fifty-one, concluding a life largely spent unemployed, Moose, then not quite twenty-six, was convinced his own days were numbered and that the best thing he could do with what little time he had left was to save mankind from itself. He had been educated by Jesuits, received a master's from St. Louis University in psychiatric social work, and even spent some months in a seminary. He thus felt reasonably prepared to embark on a career of doing good. And his old neighborhood in north St. Louis, the Holy Name Parish, had taught him certain values — such as loyalty, competitiveness, and fear of strangers — that the good fathers may have overlooked. So, except for a couple of years working for newspapers, Moose spent the first twenty years of his adult life laboring for worthy causes. He did social work. He tended to the mentally ill at a psychiatric hospital. He raised money for Catholic charities. He was the alumni secretary at his alma mater. He worked for municipal poverty programs. He was employed by the urban coalition. He was a campaign director for the liberal presidential candidate Fred Harris. And he never held any of these jobs much longer than a year or two. Most of the time he was broke, himself a victim of the poverty he worked so selflessly to eradicate.

The parish had been a universe unto itself, a sort of walled community isolated from surrounding hostile neighborhoods. "When you crossed the boundaries," says Moose, "you were out of your territory. It was a Maginot Line mentality. If we invaded somebody else's territory, they chased us back. If they got into ours, we did the same thing to them. Mine was a little world of eight square blocks. Everybody there knew everybody else and everybody outside was a stranger. I never saw any blacks. I never knew an Italian. Chinese were completely foreign to me. I'd never even eaten in a Chinese restaurant. There was a Jewish merchant in the neighborhood, and I don't know how he survived. Gravois Avenue was the Hindenburg Line separating us from the Germans. I saw no reason to cross it. We stayed in our own playgrounds and went to our own movie theaters. I was well into my teens before I ever went to a movie outside the neighborhood, and even then I felt nervous and uncomfortable. It was a restricted life. On the other hand, I got a stability there, a point of view. It gave me a sense of belonging, a feeling of security. And it gave me some values. A phony couldn't survive in our crowd. I learned early that you can't go around cheating people, that you don't get something for nothing. There was no room there for con artists. To this day, I can smell a phony a mile away. Friendship was very important to us. In our world, if you hurt somebody, you paid for it. There was no way to escape your punishment. I don't think I've ever really overcome that parochialism. I'm still wary of strangers, and it's very difficult for me to work with people who don't have a value system, who don't believe in things."

There was one place outside the neighborhood that was visited regularly as if it were a shrine. That place was Sportsman's Park, where the beloved Cardinals and the largely ignored Browns played. Moose grew up worshiping the Cardinals' Gas House Gang teams of the mid-thirties, the teams of Frankie Frisch, Ducky Medwick, Pepper Martin, and the Deans, Dizzy and Daffy. He was particularly fascinated with the Cards' veteran shortstop Leo Durocher, who played with uncommon verve and ferocity. "I was fascinated with him," says Moose. "I'd watch him raging in the dugout, cursing the umpires." Durocher was a man who believed in something, winning, with all his heart. Moose's fixation with this fierce player and, later, dictatorial and argumentative manager, will surprise no one on Moose's own Washington Square Bar & Grill softball team. Indeed, Moose, the charming *bon vivant* and cordial restaurant host, becomes a ridiculous parody of his old idol on the softball diamond. No matter that his opponents and his own players are middle-aged gentlemen looking beyond the game at hand to the party that will follow, this Durocher-manqué fights for every inch. An uninitiated spectator might logically conclude that the raging madman they see before them is surely kidding. Not on your life. "Very few people in our neighborhood won laurels outside," Moose explains. "Baseball was our window to a bigger world. So every game we played was for keeps. It all seemed so much bigger than a mere game, and when it started it became a matter of life and death. Even now, when I go out on a field, I say to myself, 'We must win!' " True. All too true.

In 1942, Moose went to work for the Cardinals as an usher and scorecard salesman. Mostly, he just watched the games. And in the World Series that year, he contrived to watch most of the home games from a seat he had staked out for himself, acting very official, in the Cardinals' dugout. He was living a dream. In the years since, he has traveled in Europe and Asia; been a confidant to at least two presidential candidates, Harris and Walter Mondale; known men of great wealth and importance; dined with famous actors and writers; and become something of a celebrity himself, but that time spent in a World Series dugout remains for him his finest hours.

Drafted into the army after graduation from St. Louis U., he was sent to Munich, where in 1955 and 1956 he was assigned to a support group for a Special Forces unit. In his free time, which was most of the time, he traveled to Paris and Rome, places that might as well have been on another planet only a few years earlier. He fell in love with Italy, particularly with Italian food, and began plotting ways to get back there somehow after his release from military duty. One thing was certain: he was finished with St. Louis.

But not right away. He returned to school for his master's after getting out of the army, and he worked part-time as a stringer and rewrite man for the *St. Louis Post Dispatch* and as an alumni director for the university. It was about this time, the late fifties, that a part of town known as Gaslight Square became *the* place to be. New nightclubs were springing up there that headlined jazz and sophisticated comedy. The people who lived and worked there were hip and bohemian. Moose, the cloistered neighborhood guy, initially resisted all attempts by friends to bring him there. He was repelled, he said, by the prevailing aura of pseudosophistication. "To me, it was a place where people were trying a little too hard to be eccentric." Europe had not changed him that much. But in the end, his curiosity got the better of him and he went down to Gaslight Square to have a look around. He would meet two strangers there who would drastically alter the course of his life.

Mary Etta Presti was job hunting when she ran across a most unusual ad placed in the *St. Louis Post Dispatch*. A family named Landesman, according to the classified, was looking for some poor soul to work excruciatingly long hours at several difficult jobs for minuscule pay. Mary Etta, a recent and unemployed graduate of Washington University, was impressed by such cheek. She answered the ad and discovered that the Landesmans had a silk-screen printing operation, a fancy antique gallery where Liberace himself bought his chandeliers, and a Gaslight Square cabaret called the Crystal Palace. Variety of this sort was hard to find. Mary Etta took the job. "It seemed more interesting than collecting unemployment, even though it paid less."

In the long run, the Crystal Palace took up most of her time. She worked as an assistant to Theodore "Ted" Flicker, who produced shows there and would eventually become somewhat better known as one of the creators of the television show "Barney Miller." Jay and his wife, Fran Landesman, were themselves talented persons actively involved in the arts. She, the former Frances Deitsch, wrote the lyrics for such jazz tunes as "Spring Can Really Hang You Up the Most" and "The Ballad of the Sad Young Men." Jay was a writer and the publisher (Neurotica Publishing Company) in his New York days of Ginsberg, William Burroughs, and John Clellan Holmes. Together, the Landesmans wrote a play, *The Nervous Set*. The Crystal Palace was their showplace for such rising young artists as Barbra Streisand, Jerry Stiller and Anne Meara, Mike Nichols, Elaine May, and Alan Arkin. Nichols, May, and Arkin, refugees from the Chicago comedy group Second City, formed their own company, the Compass Theater, in St. Louis.

Flicker and Mary Etta also booked such jazzmen as Dizzy Gillespie and Horace Silver into the place, as well as a rising young comedian named Woody Allen. Playing his first dates outside New York and suffering from the disorientation common to native New Yorkers off their turf, Allen found a friend in Mary Etta, who often cooked dinner for him in her apartment. But Mary Etta then was hardly the gourmet chef she is today, and after one particularly combustible meal, Allen looked up from his plate and inquired, "Is it true you can get polio from eating chili?" Mary Etta was every performer's best audience at the Crystal Palace, but her convulsive high-C laugh, actually more of a horror-movie shriek, was so intrusive that Landesman frequently had to ask her to take it outside.

Just up the street from the Crystal Palace was another plush club, the Golden Eagle, which was run by Fran Landesman's brother, an acerbic New Yorker named Sam Deitsch, and his partner Herb Glazer. Now both members of the extended Landesman clan, Mary Etta and Sam approached each other warily at first. "I walked into that Gaslight Square scene from a protected life," says Mary Etta. "The convent schools hadn't taught any courses on something called Sam Deitsch. I had never met anybody who talked like that or acted like that. He had a witty New York rudeness to him that I'd never experienced. God knows what abrasive thing he used as a substitute for 'How do you do?' when we first met. But we went on from there. I was very fond of him from the first minute. I monitored his romances. I listened to his social commentary. I still do. The Deitsch perspective retains to this day its great amusement value. And Sam taught me something I needed to learn back then. For all of his clipped style, he has an extraordinary tolerance for people's faults. He may appear impatient, but he is actually a very tolerant person. He made me realize that we all do unforgivable things to each other all the time."

Sam Deitsch had been on his way to San Francisco in 1957 when he stopped off in St. Louis to visit his older sister, Fran. He had gotten the San Francisco bug from his father, a wealthy and well-traveled New York garment manufacturer who considered the city by the bay to be the most civilized anywhere. He was perhaps equally inspired by the tales of amatory conquest in "Frisco" he'd heard from seamen he met in New York bars. He was convinced long before he ever clapped eyes on the place that San Francisco was his kind of town. Besides, though he was raised in comparative wealth and comfort, Sam had few aspirations in common with his crowd. He was, he figured, just about the only kid in his class from the exclusive Horace Mann School for

Boys who didn't go on to college. He tried for a time to join the family business, but he found the shadow of his father "writ large" and soon abandoned the fashion trade for the more exhilarating life of the pub crawler. This was another passion he inherited from his father. "My old man was not a drinker but he adored saloons, and I got the feel for them from him." Sam even worked in a few midtown bars before deciding once and for all to make the move west. On the way, he'd say hello to Sis in St. Louis. "I just dropped in for dinner and stayed nine years."

He got caught up, of course, in *la vie* Landesman and partially on money borrowed from the family bought into his own place, the Golden Eagle, which became an instant success. One prophetic day, a newcomer to the neighborhood, Ed Moose, wandered in for a drink with another man Sam knew. Ed ordered one of the Eagle's enormous martinis and settled in for a long afternoon. Sam sidled up to him, and the two future partners instantly fell into conversation that roamed swiftly from show business to politics to good books to local characters they mutually detested. Sam recognized a like-minded soul. "Here was this big, tall Irishman who was very funny, sucking up my martinis as if they were glasses of ice water. I realized I had a pal here, a formidable gin-drinker with good taste. He became a fixture in the place. And he finally moved into the neighborhood."

Mary Etta, in fact, showed Moose an apartment in a building owned by the Landesmans. "It looked like the set in a Beckett play," Ed recalls. "And there was a black cat that went with the place. I hated cats. It was $125 a month for approximately one room, and I'd been paying $75 for three rooms that were once occupied by Tennessee Williams in his St. Louis period. I thought these Landesman people were all robbers. Here they were putting me away in one room with a cat I hated. I figured Mary Etta was part of a cabal to do God knows what to me."

Mary Etta recalls first meeting Ed at a party Sam invited him to at the home of a mutual friend in the neighborhood, a muralist. Sam describes their meeting as a classic case of love at first sight. "Edward was charming," says Mary Etta, who may be the only person besides Margaret Moose, his mother, to call this man Edward. "I was quite taken with him. There was something about him I hadn't seen or experienced. He filled me with an unfamiliar curiosity, a curiosity I felt I had to satisfy. Thank God for that time he spent in Rome. That, at least, exposed him to things Italian."

Ed was so taken with things Italian, in fact, that he returned to Rome in 1960 as an Associated Press correspondent for the Olympic Games. He covered subjects alien to him, such as yachting ("I didn't know what a yacht was," he once said), and worked nights, often till dawn, on the rewrite desk. He interviewed the Russian female shot-putter, Tamara Press, and he watched a sleek young boxer named Cassius Clay win a gold medal. He stayed on in Rome after the Olympics working for the *Rome Daily American*. "It was $150 a month and all you could hustle. The trouble was, I couldn't hustle all that well." But this was the Rome of *La Dolce Vita*, and Ed, then thirty-one, was a wide-eyed expatriate. He lived in a *penzione* near the Spanish Steps run by a combative old woman who "was either a communist or a fascist, depending on the argument." He stayed until his money ran out, which, to his grief, was within a year. He had to go home, but he was determined not to stay there long. Instead, he would press on to that most Mediterranean of American cities, San Francisco.

He did stop off in his home town long enough to say good-bye to his friends, Mary Etta and Sam. By now, however, Mary Etta was something more than just a friend. "Edward came back extolling the virtues of San Francisco," she says. "He told me there was a spot there just waiting for me." Actually, she was ready to go. "At Gaslight Square things were beginning to run down. The neighborhood was definitely changing."

Ed got a job in San Francisco as the public-relations director for Catholic Charities and in the spring of 1961, "I put everything I owned in a Volkswagen and headed west on Route 66." The job didn't pay much, but it did give him a speedy entree into his new city. His PR predecessor and mentor, Phil Sinnott, was a former newspaperman who introduced his protégé to all the media strongholds: Breens, Jerry & Johnny's, Hanno's. Moose made contacts that would in the next decade prove invaluable in his incarnation as fledgling restaurateur.

He left Catholic Charities at the conclusion of his one-year contract, convinced by now that he had to shake himself free from the church. He caught on as a PR man for something called the National Office of Management Associations. But he didn't last long there either, sensing that his employers were less than sophisticated when, acting on his suggestion that they endow a chair at Stanford University, they dispatched an underling on a shopping tour of furniture stores. Mary

Etta had by this time joined him. She had gotten work in San Francisco as a theatrical publicist, a job that, considering the quality of her clients, had certain drawbacks of its own. "On my thirty-third birthday, I found myself writing a release, with tears streaming down my cheeks, for a performance of *Rain* that starred Carol Doda, the stripper, as Sadie Thompson." But she *was* with Ed. "He picked me up in a taxi, and we've been together ever since." Moose's recollection of their romance is only slightly more restrained. "She arrived, and I took her out as a matter of courtesy. We went to Vanessi's, then to the waterfront, and to Coit Tower. We never left North Beach, and we fell in love. We started living together that year." They were married in December 1964.

By 1966, Sam had once again run out of things to do, this time in St. Louis. Gaslight Square had "taken on a gaudy, shabby aspect." Time now, he knew, to complete his interrupted trip to the West Coast. He'd been a frequent visitor to the Moose household in San Francisco, anyway, "zapping out there" for weekend pub crawls whenever possible. "We'd do them all. The Black Cat was still open then. We'd go there and to Shanty Malone's, Jack's, Tadich's, the House of Shields, Jerry & Johnny's, Breen's, the B.V. I loved the place. I'd always intended to move there, anyway, and now my two best chums were living there." Sam sold the Golden Eagle and made his move. He lived for the next eight years in happy North Beach retirement, dabbling in real estate some, but mostly living off the money he'd realized from the sale of the Golden Eagle. He and Ed would have occasional late-night talks about getting back into the saloon business together, but in the morning most of the conversation had mercifully been forgotten.

Still, Sam was getting restless again, and, with the reelection of Richard Nixon in 1972, Ed had finally soured on good works. "All the things I believed in were either running out of gas, getting corrupted, or just plain being stopped." The boys were vulnerable to the right kind of deal.

It was about this time that Sam came across in his nightly North Beach explorations a dingy, virtually windowless little bar next door to a tropical fish aquarium on Powell Street near Union, just across Columbus Avenue from Washington Square and the magnificent spires of St. Peter and St. Paul Cathedral. The place was called Pistola's, in honor of a previous owner who, as protection against robbers and obstreperous drunks, packed a pistol in his waistband. Pistola's was then owned by a feisty North Beach character named Rose Evangelisti and her somewhat more subdued husband, Fred. Sam, unaccountably, liked the place and made it one of his regular stops. One late night when the two of them were the only ones left in the joint, Rose told Sam that she and Fred were thinking about selling out. "You should sell to me and Ed," he suggested. "You're drunk," said Rose. "True," replied Sam, "but we can talk about it in the morning when I'm not."

Sam called Ed the next day and suggested he take a look at the place. Ed was appalled by what he saw. "It looked like the girls' volleyball gym back in the Holy Name Parish." Ed talked to his accountant, George Fong. "You'll never make it there," Fong advised. "There's no parking. The place looks awful. Don't do it." Besides, Ed told Sam, almost cruelly, "Everybody I know in the saloon business is either broke, alcoholic, divorced, or all three."

Still, they could get Pistola's for only $25,000, and the monthly rent for the building was just $300. Mary Etta was asked to look the place over. She saw possibilities. The view of the park could be quite nice with windows somewhere. Ed looked at her quizzically, then stepped outside for a much-needed breath of fresh air. Then he saw the light. "I suddenly realized what a beautiful setting this actually was . . . the trees in the park across the street, Telegraph Hill rising up in all its glory. . . . I also knew I needed a job."

Sam still had some money left from his retirement bundle, and Ed knew he could borrow from a rich friend he'd met in the Harris campaign, the Wall Street investment banker Herbert Allen. And Frank and Donato Rossi, who owned Gino & Carlo's bar a few blocks away on Green Street, were interested in joining them as minority — forty percent — partners. Ed and Sam told the Evangelistis they had a deal. Things had moved so swiftly, Ed's normally calculating mind was in a whirl. "It was craziness," he said. "With no real idea what we were doing, we bought the joint."

"I don't know how we got so cocky," said Mary Etta, "but we just knew we could do it."

"Hey Glenn. Glenn Dorenbush. Over here. Join us for a minute."

Dorenbush walks with measured stride to the table. He smiles crookedly and takes a seat.

"What'll it be, Glenn?"

"I will have a Budweiser, thank you."

"Sure thing. I think you know everybody here. What's happening?"

"I have been to the Bus Stop, to Perry's, and the movies. Blue Velvet was the movie. I recommend it strongly. It has some nice perverse moments."

"We were just going to have some lunch. Join us?"

Suddenly, Dorenbush's round face is a mask of indignation. He takes a long pull from his beer and slowly rises.

"Lunch? No thank you. I do not eat. We alcoholics never eat. It is a hard and fast rule. Thank you for the beer. I've gotta get going. There are other stops."

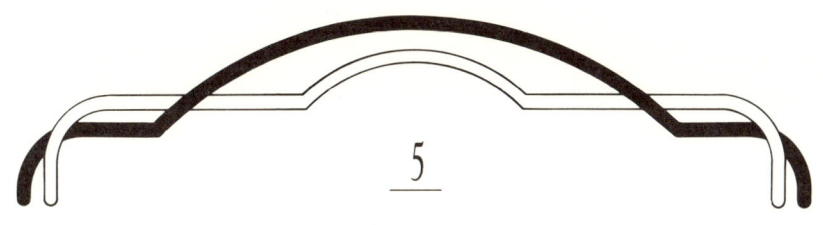

5

Calling Doctor Dorenbush

The place still looked and, yes, smelled like a girls' volleyball gym when the new owners took over. And they weren't certain among themselves what it should finally look like. The Rossis wanted a traditional North Beach Italian restaurant, stolid and folksy with checkered tablecloths and a bottle of inexpensive wine on every table. Ed and Sam had in mind a typical New York saloon with a long bar and a short menu. Architecturally, at least, the majority owners prevailed. Pure chance would pretty much resolve the culinary issue.

The first priority was opening up the little building to expose customers to the sylvan view of the park across the street. The trouble was, there was only six thousand dollars to spend on renovation. Ed turned to his friends the Eden twins, Tom and Ted, two young architects who had opened their own office five years earlier. Ed had met them before that at Jerry & Johnny's, the newspaper hangout. Ted was a regular there with his boss of the time, Joe McCarthy, and he assumed that Ed was just another newspaperman. The Edens had come to San Francisco in 1963 after graduating from the University of Miami in Florida and doing advance study at the Frank Lloyd Wright Foundation in Scottsdale, Arizona. Tall, blond, and identically good-looking, they soon became popular men about town, dapper young yachtsmen who achieved some national recognition when they bought Humphrey Bogart's old yawl, *Santana*, in the early seventies. They accepted The

Square job as a challenge. "We're like plastic surgeons," said Ted Eden. "We usually see things when they're at their worst. And this place looked bad, like a cave with little slits for windows. It looked like what it had been: a North Beach speakeasy."

The Edens were asked to design a room that looked as if it had not been designed at all. It was to have a spare and uncluttered look, and under no circumstances was it to have any of the characteristics of the "fern bars" that seemed to be sprouting like weeds all over San Francisco at the time. Since the tropical fish aquarium next door had not yet been acquired by the new owners, the Edens were handicapped initially by a lack of space. But they gamely plunged ahead, accepting as payment for their efforts $860 in cash and a year's free dining and drinking. In place of the slits, the Edens installed large oriole windows facing the street. They put Dutch doors at the entrance (which later changed), a striped awning above, and above the awning they painted in bold white letters against a blue background: Washington Square Bar & Grill. In a rush of sentiment, they painted a red rose on the sign as a tribute to the previous owner, Rose Evangelisti. In 1973, there was not another "bar & grill" in the San Francisco telephone directory.

For years Sam had carried a small, dark-brown paint chip in his wallet. He would withdraw it at times he considered appropriate and say, "This, my friends, is the color a bar should be." When it came time to consider The Square's interior, he showed the chip to Shirley Osumi, the Edens' interior designer. "No," said Shirley, "that's not the color a bar should be. This is." And she withdrew from her purse another chip, painted a peculiar shade of rust. "You're right," said Sam. And that became the dominant color inside. Mary Etta called it smoky grape. It is a subtle and yet distinctive shade, and it seemed to capture the mood of subdued gaiety the new owners hoped would infuse their little bar.

The logo, depicting a barman uncorking a bottle of champagne from which an ampersand spurts forth, was designed by Larry Green, a well-known North Beach illustrator and designer. It appears now on match covers, cocktail napkins, and all Square newsletters and publications, of which there are surprisingly many.

Finding a proper bar was a trickier proposition. The bar at Pistola's was made of cheap plywood and was far too tacky for what Ed and Sam had in mind. Ed prowled through antique stores and junkyards and was a regular at auctions in his quest for material to build the impressive structure he envisioned. He knew that this was an issue of some consequence, since every saloon in San Francisco of any stature had a showcase bar. The Templebar's ornate masterwork had come around the Horn at the time of the Gold Rush; Breen's bar was reputedly the longest in the world. Moose had begun to despair of finding something remotely competitive when, on a hunch, he dropped in one morning at a warehouse on Battery Street that he knew had just received a large shipment of antiques from England. Among the odds and ends there was a large and presumably useless pile of wood from a recently demolished London office of Barclay's Bank. "It was just discarded stuff," says Ed, "but it was good wood, French walnut eight to ten inches thick, and I could get it all for under a thousand dollars. I took it." He had his bar.

But what about the grill? The Rossis were still holding out for an Italian menu. Sam and Ed were committed to what they called "the saloon concept," burgers and fries. It wasn't that the majority partners disliked Italian food. On the contrary, they ate it almost nightly. Ed had developed a taste for that cuisine during his Rome period, and Sam had been eating in Italian restaurants for much of his life. And as residents now of North Beach, they lived with the aroma of garlic and pasta. One of their favorite places, in fact, had been Swiss Louie's on Broadway, an old-fashioned Italian restaurant of the sort the Rossis had in mind as a model for the new place. In time, Ed and Sam became friendly with Swiss Louie's chef, Aldo Persich. Born in Trieste, Persich had run away from home at fifteen and gone to sea, where he learned to cook. It was a brutal internship of sixteen-hour days in cramped and steamy galleys, and in time he tired of it. He finally jumped ship in San Francisco and found work in restaurants all over North Beach. He had been the head chef at Swiss Louie's since 1961. His tenure there was characterized by continuous disputes with the owner, John Marsachino, some of which culminated in firings and walkouts. But none was serious enough to keep Aldo out of the kitchen for long.

As friends of the combatants, Ed and Sam were quietly amused by these tiffs. There were too many of them to take seriously. Then one afternoon Ed ran into Aldo at the bar in Gino & Carlo's. The cook was in his usual high dudgeon. "I quit, Ed. I am finished at Swiss Louie's." "Sure, Aldo, sure." "No, this is serious. I want to work for you and Sam." Still convinced that this was yet another temporary bustup, Ed suggested he come on down to The Square that day. Even if Aldo went back, as expected, to Swiss Louie's, at least he could help set up the kitchen at The Square. Aldo walked in, rolled up his sleeves, and at one sitting ordered from memory thirteen hundred food items from the suppliers. And then he set about preparing a menu. An Italian menu. "Presto, change-o," said Sam. "We are a full-tilt boogie Italian restaurant." Aldo did not return to Swiss Louie's. He stayed on at The Square another six years, until his final retirement, and set the culinary tone of the place. In a sense, he is still there; his photograph hangs in a prominent place behind the bar, the only member of the staff, past or present, so honored.

The Washington Square Bar & Grill opened unobtrusively for business the day after Labor Day in 1973, even though carpenters and plumbers were still hammering away inside. "We didn't know what the hell we were doing," said Ed. "And wood was flying everywhere." "There were guys sitting at the bar with humongous hangovers," Sam recalls, "and the noise was killing them." By December 14, the remodeling was reasonably complete, so an official opening was staged. It was a disaster. The Pacific Gas & Electric Company didn't turn the gas on in time, and the food was not delivered. Customers peeked in out of curiosity and left almost immediately, usually without even ordering a drink. Nobody knew or cared who the owners were. "Basically," says Sam, "we were the unknown brothers." And when the last customer filed unhappily out, the two majority owners repaired to the kitchen where they got royally drunk and had an argument that nearly severed their relationship. Sam wondered why-oh-why he had ever gotten back in the business, and Ed began to think that do-gooding wasn't so bad after all.

At the same time they were assembling, both by accident and by design, a remarkable cast of characters. Their first waiter, Dennis MacKey, was virtually deaf. He took orders by reading lips and answered summonses out of instinct and anticipation. And yet he was the soul of efficiency and waiterly integrity. Mary Etta recalls him chasing after customers who had left too much change on the table, apparently rejecting the possibility that the excess was intended as a generous tip. Dennis also established the employees' dress code when he advised the owners that he worked best in a tuxedo and not in the more casual attire suggested to him. Square waiters ever since have dressed in formal evening attire and waitresses in black and white facsimiles.

The day bartender, Deno Petrucci, was a typical North Beach character, a familiar figure in coffeehouse card games. The night bartender, Toody Buchart, was a jazz drummer. The second waiter, Rudy Lorenz, also known as Rudy Runamok, was in Moose's charitable estimation "a ferocious drunk" who was not averse to slipping out for a quick belt down the street between orders. The third waiter, Peter Yeung, had worked with Rudy Runamok in the Fairmont Hotel's Tonga Room, a restaurant laid out around an indoor swimming pool and meant to suggest a South Seas island, complete with nightly tropical storms. Yeung came to The Square as a responsible family man, a hard-working immigrant from Hong Kong. He was invariably pleasant and efficient despite a language handicap, but in time his own weakness, gambling, began to take hold of him. He became a big man in Chinatown gambling circles, touring the main drag, Grant Avenue, in rented limousines. He entertained lavishly, once throwing back-to-back Christmas parties for his colleagues on the day and night shifts at The Square. Alas, as with all gamblers, his luck did not hold. His debts mounted seriously, and when two disagreeable-looking gentlemen from Las Vegas made inquiries about him in the restaurant one day, Peter saw that the jig was up. He has not been seen since by anyone at The Square. Speculation has it that the waiter was too wily for the Vegas hoods and, succored by the Chinatown underground, has safely made his way back to Hong Kong, where he is presumably prospering as the proprietor of a *pai gow* emporium. That, at least, is the wishful thinking of his old friends down at The Square.

As the bar began finally to assume some form and purpose, it became obvious that the aquarium next door would have to be flushed out. The Square had acquired lease to it shortly after opening, but the proprietors seemed in no rush to vacate. They finally did in the summer of 1974 after, says Ed, "We threatened the biggest Friday-night fish fry in San Francisco history." The Edens now had some room to work with and they set about converting a little bar into at least a medium-sized restaurant. The enlarged capacity had its own drawback, though. What if nobody came? Lord knows, the bar itself wasn't doing all that well. Passersby would scarcely feel impelled to come inside if all they could see through the large windows was a vacant room. So the Edens included in their new design draperies that would separate the bar from the new dining room and, in fact, partition the dining room into smaller rooms. Now, if nobody came, people outside would at least be spared the dispiriting sight of empty tables.

The place was, in effect, finished, but the dispute with the Rossis was not. The Square was taking a form not entirely congenial to the brothers. True, it had, by virtue of Aldo's unexpected arrival, become an Italian restaurant, and in the first months it had been pretty much a neighborhood joint. But Ed and Sam had much broader ambitions. They were determined that The Square should become, in Mary Etta's words, "a lively bistro," a meeting place for the movers and shakers and chroniclers of San Francisco life. Donato and Frank Rossi could not keep pace with this sort of thinking. And they had the additional problem of trying to remain active in two bars. Frank, the younger of the two by thirteen years, found the double work life particularly exhausting. There were days when he would arrive at Gino & Carlo's at five in the morning to prepare for the six o'clock opening (customers there are notorious for early imbibing) and then bustle down the hill and across Columbus Avenue to fill in as the lunchtime maître d' at The Square. It was a punishing schedule, and in time, it wore thin.

The Rossis are affable men, intelligent and fair-minded, but the volatile Moose and the mercurial Deitsch soon taxed their patience. They agreed on little. Jazz lovers Ed and Sam had, for example, decided the place should have live music. Donato and Frank thought the noise would disturb the diners. A pianist was hired. Bill Tennent played an odd repertoire of Mozart and ragtime, and he never talked, either to the customers or his employers. One night Bobby Riggs, the former tennis champion turned tennis hustler, came into the joint. Riggs is a garrulous sort who hates eating alone. He asked Ed if the pianist might join him on his next break. Ed said he certainly could, and he and Riggs got on famously. "They were a perfect pair," Ed recalls. "One never stopped talking and the other never said a word. Riggs told me afterward he'd never enjoyed a dinner conversation more."

The piano would not become an important feature of The Square, however, until Burt Bales began playing it there in 1975. Bales is a San Francisco jazz legend, a brilliant pianist in the Jelly Roll Morton manner, who was also a heroic drinker. There were nights at Pier 23, a waterfront saloon where he played for more than a dozen years, when in the middle of a magnificent set Bales would slip slowly off his piano stool onto the sawdust floor. He had pretty much disappeared from the local scene in the early seventies, and it was assumed, not without reason, that he had simply wandered off to some hovel to die. Moose discovered through Robin Hodes, a mutual friend and a musician himself, that Bales was alive and, though not well, still in San Francisco. At Moose's urging, Bales agreed to play a couple of nights a week at the new bar. Word got out among the jazzman's legion of fans, and the place was soon packed on his nights at the piano. Bales hadn't stopped drinking completely, but he had slowed down enough so that most of the time he made it to his gigs at The Square on time. And he liked it there because there were some familiar faces in the room and much of the crowd was genuinely interested in his music. Bales played there regularly for nine years. Moose now saw the possibilities of employing recognized talent, so he next hired Norma Teagarden, younger sister of trombonist Jack and trumpeter Charlie and an accomplished jazz pianist in her own right. Now in her late seventies, Norma still plays there, and because she is a lure to younger musicians, a small band seems to assemble around her on her nights. Moose also hired, in 1978, Mike Lipskin, one of the few remaining masters of the stride piano style first made popular by such as Willie "The Lion" Smith and Fats Waller. On other nights Dick Fregulia, a somewhat more modern stylist, and Ray Skjelbred play. Skjelbred is usually joined by the brilliant clarinetist and soprano saxophonist Dick Hadlock. There is jazz in The Square seven nights a week and sometimes twice on Sundays. The music the Rossis initially opposed has been a prime source of the place's immense popularity.

The Square's pianists occupy a unique position in the barroom. They play atop a slightly raised platform, and they face away from the audience directly into the wall. This seating arrangement has the distinct advantage of discouraging the overserved or overeager customer from pestering the musicians, since a pianist with his back to the audience seems somehow less accessible. Moose said he had no choice in positioning the piano because there was no room for it anywhere else. As a small concession to ordinary human intercourse, a large mirror has been hung above the piano so that performer and audience may at least see each other in reflection.

There is another mirror, much larger and more ornate, hanging in back of the bar, that affords tipplers a rare view of the entire room. The appearance of an attractive woman in the doorway occasions no unseemly head-swiveling in the Washington Square Bar & Grill; the discreet imbiber has only to look straight ahead into the mirror to take in the whole scene. The mirror sees all, and during the course of an average day, a remarkable parade passes in review before its glassy stare.

The original mirror behind the bar, installed in 1978, was much less impressive than the current model, and it was not welcomed by all as a triumph of interior decoration. "What is this piece of voyeuristic bullshit?" bartender Tom Slater inquired at first sight of it. Slater's objections, as it develops, were not entirely based on aesthetic considerations. "Tom had a little bald spot on the back of his head," recalls Riofski, his fellow night barman for many years. "He's a tall man, so hardly anyone noticed. But with that mirror hanging there, everybody sitting at the bar could see it clearly. Tom was mortified. He even tried putting black shoe polish on the back of his head to disguise it."

One night after closing, Slater decided to take action against the offending artifact. Emboldened by several jolts of green Chartreuse, he cut the mirror down from the wall with a butcher knife borrowed from the kitchen and packed it upstairs to the office, placing it symbolically at the feet of the oppressor. Moose found it there the next morning. Not a word was said that day, and as time passed, Slater felt increasingly confident that he had performed a public service. Then, some six months later, as Riofski remembers the occasion, "Tom and I came to work and found this monstrous two-thousand-pound job over the bar. It was just about the biggest mirror either of us had ever seen. It was as if Ed and Sam were telling Tom, 'OK, pal, let's see you take this one down.'" Slater never tried, and, in fact, the mirror outlasted him behind the bar.

The Rossis, meanwhile, decided to sell their share of the place. The brothers had been true assets in the early stages of the operation when, as Mary Etta has said, "we needed that fine Genovese spirit," but their philosophical differences with Ed and Sam had widened and their influence had declined. They were also finding it physically impossible keeping two such different bars functioning. "People at our own place were beginning to wonder where we were all the time," said Frank Rossi. Sam and Ed agreed to buy them out. Unfortunately, they could not agree on a fair price. Sam and Ed suggested the Rossis be repaid their original investment of twenty thousand dollars. Donato and Frank wanted considerably more, as much as one hundred thousand dollars. Eventually, attorney and arbitrator Sam Kagel decided that the original investment plus normal bank interest was the fair price, and both sides agreed.

Ed and Sam were now the sole proprietors, but their dispute with the popular and established Rossis had cost them dearly in neighborhood goodwill. Charles McCabe, a Gino & Carlo's regular and a *Chronicle* columnist second only to Caen in popularity at the time, remained convinced to his dying day that the Rossis had been cheated. Although he had been one of The Square's earliest and most valuable customers, he now virtually boycotted the place. And McCabe, a man of incalculable wrath and considerable influence, was not a good enemy to have. He continued to have his first ale of the day — usually at eight in the morning — at Gino & Carlo's, but he avoided The Square, ordinarily his second stop of the morning, as if it were the mess hall of a leper colony.

But McCabe, unlike Caen, was not given to mentioning his favorite or least favorite saloons by name in his columns, so Ed and Sam were mercifully spared a public flogging over the lamentable Rossi affair. And the Rossis were not the sort to hold grudges. Peace was soon achieved, threatened only when, in 1983, Ed and Sam neglected to mention the Rossis in a special publication they distributed marking The Square's tenth anniversary. But far from being envious of their former partners' success, the Rossis maintain they are well out of the deal. "We have no regrets," says Frank Rossi. "Being out of there is more of a relief than anything. With the two places, we were in a Catch-22 situation."

The Square was hardly an instant success. Its odd location, beyond the North Beach mainstream and on the outskirts of downtown, made it seem inaccessible both to the business community and to the neighborhood layabouts. Besides, there was no parking. The bar, however, did attract some influential local characters. John Wasserman, the eccentric and brilliantly funny *Chronicle* pop music and "bad movie" critic, was an early supporter and the first customer to bring in visiting celebrities. "Whatever you do," he once told Ed in one of the co-owner's moments of despair, "keep this place open. I like it."

The Square was getting something of a reputation as a talker's hangout, but the business volume wasn't there. "Nobody was coming in," says Moose. "We were doing so poorly we were barely paying the bills. We had had some critical success, but there were so many restaurants in North Beach we were being lost in the shuffle."

They were rescued by one of San Francisco's most unusual and, in his own mad way, influential personalities. In a city that takes an inordinate pride in its characters, Glenn Dorenbush still stands apart. His roots, surprisingly, are in Middle America. He was born in Grand Rapids, Michigan, and was educated at both Michigan State and the University of Michigan, where without any particular enthusiasm or purpose he attended but declined to finish law school. He worked for a few years in a Chicago public-relations firm; then, finding regular employment alien to his expansive and fun-loving nature and buoyed by a small inheritance, he moved to San Francisco in 1959 when he was twenty-nine. And he never, by any conventional definition, worked again. What Dorenbush did in San Francisco was go to bars. His rounds would begin at 9:30 in the morning and conclude when the bars closed at 2:00 A.M. In that span he would have polished off, with little detrimental effect to his personality or equilibrium, from thirty to forty Scotch and waters. He is a moon-faced man of medium stature who dresses in the shabby-genteel tradition. He has a courtly manner, and he is never, even when deeply into his cups, noisy or unpleasant. He can be an entertaining and remarkably well-informed conversationalist when he chooses to be, but he prefers the role of observer to participant. Observing, in fact, is his one great and enduring gift. And it is the principal reason he loves saloons, for he can sit for hours beyond recall silently taking in the scene around him.

Dorenbush, in time, put his powers of observation to good use. He began jotting down notes on what he heard and saw in his travels and sending them on to the newspaper columnists, most prominently Caen. His jottings were so cleverly written that they appeared in print virtually unedited, and it soon became obvious to even the densest of saloonkeepers that having Dorenbush on the premises was professionally as well as financially advantageous. His business was soon solicited by the more ambitious barkeeps, but Dorenbush held himself to a high standard and would only go to the bars he liked. Food, of course, had no place in his considerations (he had a mortal terror of being caught eating anywhere), and so very few of the major restaurants were included in his itinerary. All he required was good drink and good company. Because his standards were well known, a bar owner fortunate enough to have Dorenbush seated on a stool for several hours had a claim of sorts to fame. Because of his professional manner and studious attention to surroundings, McCabe began calling him "Dr. Dorenbush." And no question about it, the good doctor was one of the most quoted men in town. Persons who knew him only by reputation would flock to his side hoping he would drop a pearl their way. They were, of course, almost always disappointed, for Dr. Dorenbush was no raconteur. He would smile sweetly upon those who invaded his privacy and say nothing.

Perry Butler, a fugitive from the New York advertising community, was the first saloonkeeper to take full advantage of the doctor's talents. When he opened his Union Street bar, Perry's, he quickly hired Dorenbush as the house public-relations man. Dorenbush, however, rejected the term "public relations" out of hand, preferring instead to call himself "one of the last survivors of a noble breed, a publicity agent." In no time, Dorenbush's columnar *bon mots* made Perry's one of the hottest spots in town.

Ed and Sam had met Dorenbush years before in the old Buena Vista Cafe, and when The Square opened, they naturally invited him in for a drink. He cheerfully obliged them, and though, typically, he said nothing, he apparently liked what he saw. One day, another slow one, he ambled over to Moose and, as Mary Etta recalls the signal occasion, said from beneath half-lidded eyes, "I like this place." From that moment on, The Square had it made. "Glenn started coming in every day," said Ed. "And he brought other people with him, some of the Perry's crowd, a lot of newspapermen." Items began to appear in Caen's column, and Caen himself soon began dropping in. It was Dorenbush who first suggested that jazz would be appropriate background music (though he was initially opposed to the piano) for the kind of crowd The Square was attracting. "He was working for Perry's at the time, and we couldn't afford to pay him anything, but it didn't seem to make any difference to him," says Ed. "He had adopted us, and if Glenn Dorenbush adopts you, you'll do well. We never did have any sort of formal agreement with him. It was all unspoken, but I'll tell you, Glenn

Dorenbush is a very, very important part of our history. It's the strangest thing, but he brings with him an atmosphere, an aura that is all his own. It's truly incredible."

There are various ways of knowing when you've made it. One is getting a nickname. The regulars, Dorenbush included, immediately started calling the new place The Square. Cab drivers, answering more and more requests for rides there, gave it the code name "Washbag," and Caen and some lesser columnists picked up on that, much to Moose's regret. But Sam Deitsch thinks the turning point may have been reached midway through the Dorenbush era when a woman customer rushed into the place and breathlessly reported that the driver of the Number 41 bus she had been riding had announced: "Next stop, Washington Square: Saints Peter and Paul Cathedral. Washington Square Park. And the Washington Square Bar & Grill." Now that's making it. Thank you, doctor.

"See those guys at the bar? The ones drinking white wine?"

"Yeah."

"Notice anything unusual about them?"

"No."

"Look again. You see? They aren't having any fun, that's what it is. I got this theory, see. Guys who order white wine never have any fun. For women it's OK. They're just trying to get through an evening the best way they know how. But for a guy to drink white wine, there's something wrong. The way I figure it, there's only two reasons why a guy would drink white wine at a bar. I'm not talking about with meals, you understand. A little white wine with fish is perfectly OK. But to sit at a bar and drink white wine I figure the guy must be trying to cut back. He's probably worried about his drinking, so he's easing off with a little wine, hoping he won't get shit-faced. Now, if you're worried about that, no way you can have a good time in here."

"So what's the other reason?"

"The other reason is he doesn't like to drink at all. He's uncomfortable in a saloon. Doesn't feel right there. He's happier jogging or being down at the gym.

Most of the time, he'll just order one of those stupid bottles of water. He's really whooping it up when he hits the wine. He'll never drink red, you'll notice. That looks too much like a drink. The white you can't tell from the water. So this guy can't be having any fun, either. He's ordered the white wine just so he'll have something in his hand. A guy like that is very unhappy at a bar."

"So?"

"So, we're better off without them in here. I tell you what they do to me. They depress me. In fact, I think I'll go home."

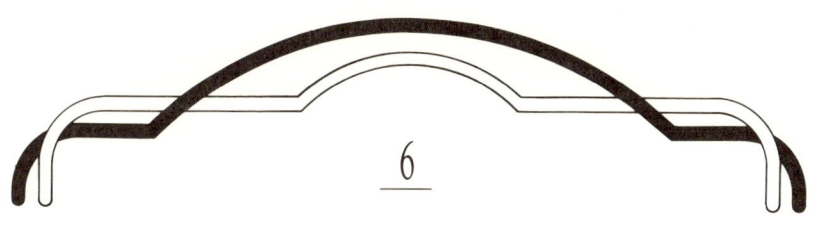

6

The Old Guard

I n The Square's formative years there were at least as many oddballs and outright crazies working there as eating and drinking there. But without these rich personalities the place would have lost much of its identity. In a sense, though most of them are gone now, they made the Washington Square Bar & Grill what it is today. But that certainly was not their intention; mostly they just needed work. And they came from everywhere. Of all those early staffers, three stand apart:

Hal

He always looked like royalty. Dressed to the nines, tall and straight, with a gray beard and thinning hair, Hal Thunes could have passed for a duke instead of The Square's first maître d' and manager. But he was no blue blood. In fact, he came to San Francisco in 1965 from Los Angeles, where he grew up, went to three colleges, and worked for a time as a jujube salesman. His life since he left The Square in 1979 after five years on the job had been a succession of illnesses and financial setbacks, but Hal's was an indomitable spirit. When his many friends in North Beach gave him a party in February 1988 at Little City, the restaurant across the street from The Square, he was there greeting guests at the door in the old regal manner. And the party recalled for him all the good times. . . .

"I guess you could say Ed is now the Toots Shor of San Francisco. He's a better restaurateur than anyone in town, but he's also a very complicated man. Charles McCabe always used to say that what bothered him most about Ed was that every time they talked, Ed seemed to be looking past him for someone more important to talk to. Well, that's just part of the business. You gotta be watching that door. Ed once told me, 'Hal, this may be just a job to you. And it may be all fun and games for Sam. But this is my retirement.'

"Ed and I never really got along that well. I was Sam's man, and he knew it. We had our differences, and a lot of them were of my making. I remember once Ed took me aside to talk about the future of the joint. He asked me what I'd do if I were running it. Now, I adore Mary Etta, but back then I thought she was rattling the place too much, creating too much paperwork. She was expanding the menu at a time I thought we had maxed out and should be looking more to consolidating our gains, cutting back a little and becoming more of a chophouse instead of a major restaurant. So he asked me what I'd do, and I said I'd get rid of Mary Etta. Ed just turned purple and told me, 'Never say anything like that again.' It turns out I was just as wrong as I could be. Mary Etta was very important. She kept up with the times, kept changing the menu to keep up. I think that little encounter contributed importantly to my deteriorating relationship with Ed.

"Then there was the time I was working behind the bar and Ed was standing back there talking to a customer. Now Ed's a big man, and every time I made a move I'd have to step around him. Finally, in exasperation, I said to him, 'Ed, would you mind standing someplace else?' Well, he gave me a look and said, 'I can stand anywhere I want. It's my place.' 'You're right,' I said, and I handed him my apron and headed for the door. He had to go out and bring me back. But you know, he never stood behind the bar again.

"I left The Square for a combination of reasons. For one thing, I was developing maître d's syndrome, the delusions of grandeur thing. What happens is that everybody on the way out of the joint thanks you for their evening, so you begin thinking you were responsible for their having a good time. And then the clientele changed dramatically. Now newspaper and union guys are usually good drinkers, but we were starting to get other kinds in there, and my tolerance for drunken lawyers and giddy stockbrokers is not high. These guys get a few drinks in them and think it gives them a license to intrude on other people. Either that or they just don't care. I think it's maybe that they concentrate on their jobs so much they don't know how to relax gracefully. One night, one of these drunken lawyers turned on some long-haired kid at the bar and said, 'Where were you in the Vietnam War? I was in the marines.' He was going to beat the kid up, so I eighty-sixed him. He came in the next day and told me that he'd closed a two-and-a-half-million-dollar deal that day and he was just celebrating. He pulled out his wallet and showed me the Father of the Year certificate he'd been awarded that year. I told him I didn't give a shit, that you just can't go around trying to beat people up in bars no matter who you are. I'll say this for Ed and Sam, they always backed me when I eighty-sixed somebody.

"Then too, you can get an inflated idea of your importance in this business. To a lot of people, you're a kind of star, and that's bullshit. They say that a bartender gets to really know his fellowman. That's bullshit too. At best he gets only a superficial idea of what anybody's like. And most of the time, we're like cops. We see only the worst side. Take that Father of the Year. All I saw was the nasty streak in him. I think you get a little wobbly in this business. Like a prizefighter, you should take a physical once a month.

"In time, you take on a proprietary interest in the place you work in. That happened to me at The Square. I began to feel like it was my place. And as Ed got more and more control of the joint, it was obvious he was looking for a younger, different type of guy out front, which was Mark. And by now, I was doing a foolish thing. I was going with somebody I worked with, Judy Berkley. I was getting to be a little like Sam Malone in "Cheers." Judy wasn't really like Diane on TV, but there was a lot of that. Anyway, it was time to move on. I trained Mark, and soon as he was ready, I was gone.

"In the years since, I've had time to think back on those times, and I know that, personal idiosyncrasies aside, I really value those two men, Ed and Sam, a lot. And I've come to realize that, aside from being an asshole on occasion, I did a lot for that place."

Slater

He was a big, tough black-haired Irishman from New York who came to San Francisco in the mid-seventies as a self-described "refugee from the West Village." He was a boozer, a brawler, a gambler, and a lover. He was also a charmer, but he could be as abrupt and uncompromising as a Barbary Coast bouncer. When Moose was asked once if there was any sort of weapon kept behind the bar in case of violent emergency, he smiled malevolently and replied, "Slater is our weapon." In his six years as a bartender there, Slater wooed more than one waitress and even married one before moving on. He spent some years running his own place on Long Island after he left The Square; moved to Sarasota, Florida, for a while; and then finally returned to San Francisco, older at fifty-odd, married again, and hoping to open his own place.

"In 1975, the place was just starting out, and it was wonderful. I loved it. What people we had there then! Now, I'm a wise guy from New York, but they were doing things in this place I couldn't believe. We got one bartender, Peter DeLucca, who comes to work packing a gun. He frightened the crap out of me. And there was Chick Arrigotti, George Yee, Maya Luckmann, Sofi Kurtz, and Hal. Now these people were into everything. What a cast of characters!

"One day, I told Chick about a bartender I used to work with up in the Jewish Alps, the Catskills. He was an old Jewish guy, and as soon as the lights went off for the show in the lounge, he'd scoop up all the change in front of him. So one night, a guy calls him on it. He demands his money be returned. The old bartender feigns outrage. 'You accuse me of cheating?' he shouts. 'Me, with my sick old mother about to die? So, you feel that way, here, take the whole tip jar. What do I care. Maybe you need it more than I do. Me, with my sick mother near death. Here, take it!' And he shoves the tip jar at the customer. Well, naturally, the customer is embarrassed by all this. Suddenly, he's made to look the bad guy. So he hands back the tip jar and gives the old bartender another fiver. Now Chick is impressed with this story, and I'll be damned if he didn't try the same routine. He scoops up some guy's change, and because he's not too smooth about it, the customer calls him on it. So Chick goes into the old Jewish bartender's spiel, just about as I'd told it to him. He pushes the tip jar at the guy and gets about as far as 'my sick old mother,' before the guy grabs the tip jar and walks out of the place. 'You know, Chick,' I tell him, 'I don't think you got that one down too good.'

"Another night Chick is not working, but he's in the place and he's got a pretty good heat on. So he gets into a beef with this big guy at the bar and it's starting to get loud. This all starts down at Neil's end of the bar, and Neil has just started working there. In those days, I used to give Neil an awful lot of shit. I resented the hell out of him. I knew he'd come into the place on a connection. A friend of his introduced him to Ed, and next thing you know, he's got a job. I used to give the poor kid so much shit, I had him in tears. But he stood up to it, even though I didn't show him a whole lot of mercy. Anyway, Neil is all upset this night because Chick is egging this guy on, and Neil knows who the guy is. So he comes up to me and says, 'We gotta do something, Tom. This guy'll kill Chick. He's a loan-shark enforcer, a leg-breaker.' So we decide to eighty-six the guy, and surprisingly, from what Neil's said, the guy is leaving without too much trouble, when Chick — oh, Chick — yells out something like, 'See ya later, asshole.' That does it. The next thing we know the guy's got Chick bent over the hood of a car out front and he looks as if he means business. Neil is jumping around saying Chick's gonna be killed. I figure I better do something quick, but I don't want to go out there with an empty hand if this guy is as tough as Neil says he is. A leg-breaker. So I grab this wrench from behind the bar, tear outside, and belt this guy right behind the ear. He goes down just like that. No more trouble. But it turns out the guy isn't quite as bad as Neil makes him out to be. And he never comes back to The Square. Instead, he tells people to stay away because the place is just too violent.

"Hal was working the floor back then, and he and I really got involved in the place. Sam and Ed were making all the command decisions, of course, but they pretty much left us alone in the place after 9:00 P.M., and we got to feeling it really was our place. We had to make all the floor decisions, the everyday decisions, like what to do with a drunk. And because we could do those things, we supposed we could do more, like decide what should be on the menu, who should be hired, things like that. After all, I'd been in the business twenty years by then and Hal about thirty. We could see a lot of things we thought they were doing wrong there, and we'd talk about them by the hour. Hal's a very sensitive man, you know, and he felt more strongly about the place than some guy who's just putting in a shift. So we'd close up at two o'clock in the morning, pull the blinds, and talk for three hours about what should be done. In the meantime, of course, we'd knock the shit out of the liquor supply, so by five or thereabouts I guess you could say our perceptions were not as clear as they might have been.

"In a way, it was very frustrating. And in time, Hal just sort of burned out. Then I did. It had been a good time, but there was nothing left for me to do. And by now the San Francisco booze bug had gotten to me. I needed to clean up my act, and San Francisco is no place to do that. The place was changing, too. It seemed to me it was ending the way the Village scene did. When I first came to The Square, it was like 1965 all over again. Life was exciting, full of meaning. Then, suddenly, just like the Village, it was different. No cannon went off or anything, it just wasn't the same. The employees, the customers, everything seemed to change. The old North Beach crowd, the people who first started coming there, were now scaring the shit out of the new people. And the new people were the ones spending the money. Now, I love Mark. Everybody does. But when people like that come in, you know things are changing. The place was getting respectable, popular. It just wasn't free-form anymore. But it had to change, didn't it? I think those of us who came in at the start had a longer run than, Lord knows, we deserved. I have no complaints."

Sofi

Sofi Kurtz was the frenetic little waitress with the big eyes and the sharp tongue. She took no guff from either customers or bosses. And like the social worker she once was, she could lecture the unruly patron ("Now sir, if you don't eat your vegetables, you won't get any dessert"). When Sofi finally quit, she became a happy customer and a regular in the otherwise all-male Thursday football pool. In a way, she still thinks of The Square as her place.

"We're sitting here at Table 42. Rudy Runamok worked out the numbering system for the tables. It was all based on one of his winning keno cards, a weird system for a restaurant. You see, we're at 42 and across from us is 18. Makes no sense, but it's so weird that it sticks with the waiters, and as far as I know, no one has ever had any trouble with it.

"I started work here on February 6, 1976. I'd met Sam earlier on the *Santana*, the Eden twins' boat. I was working at Capp's Corner up the street from The Square at the time, the only waitress there who was under forty, weighed less than five hundred pounds, and wasn't retarded. It's an Italian place, and I was trying to pass as a Sicilian Jew, but it didn't work with Mrs. Capp. I was only out of work for twelve hours when Sam hired me. I'd already worked five years as a waitress and before that I'd been a psychiatric social worker here and in New York, and that's perfect preparation for the restaurant world. I always regarded The Square as just another emergency ward. By the time I got to The Square, I was committed to being a waitress. I'd used my degree, and I think did some good in the world, so I had no regrets about getting out of social work. Besides, I'd got to the point where I didn't really need to deal with any more schizophrenics.

"It turns out I wasn't much different from anyone else on the staff here. Lucy Kendall and I started working lunch, and she was a lawyer. Everybody else was either writing a book, painting, or singing and dancing somewhere. And Ed himself had been a psychiatric social worker. I'll never forget one Christmas. Ed got the staff together and told us that the next few weeks would be rough, both physically and psychologically, for all of us and if there was anyone who didn't think he could handle it, he should just speak up and Ed would see what he could do to make it easier for him. Now that struck me as an unusually humane approach to the business.

"Besides, I was still using my training. I had a customer once who wouldn't listen to anything I said. I'd be standing there, telling him about the specials, making recommendations, and he'd be talking to everybody else at the table as if I didn't exist. Finally, I said, 'Sir, you won't let me wait on you, will you?' Then I turned to his family sitting at the table and asked, 'Is he always like this?' He was fine after that. And of course, we had people on the staff then who were seriously paranoid. There was a waiter named Cal who thought he was Ed's son. He was horrifying to work with. He screamed at everybody and he once tore one of the waitresses', Arlene's, blouse in a fit of rage. He was driving us all nuts, so Ed assigned Mark to keep an eye on him. Turned out Cal had just taken on a little too much coke for his own good. We were a pretty tolerant staff in those days. We'd all done everything: drinking, screwing, and drugs. So there wasn't much we wouldn't put up with. In fact, Ed and Sam were interested then in hiring wild men, characters, to give the place character. But Cal was too much. He had to go.

"Oh, there were others. Rudy Runamok for sure. And Helmut, who had every addiction there was. He'd been in Vietnam and was a classic tragedy of that war. Still, he had this nonstop Robin Williams type of free-association humor, and we all loved him. But it finally got to be too much for him. We were all drinking a lot then, but he'd be back with the bartenders where the serious drinking was going on. Finally he left us and joined AA to clean up his act. We gave him a big farewell party where we did parodies of all the regular customers for him. We had this one guy who came in every day named Mort Siegel. He sat on exactly the same stool for five hours every day. A crippled old lady begging for a place to sit couldn't pry him off that stool. So in one of our skits, a waiter comes out from backstage dressed like Mort with a stool attached to his ass.

"There were fights here then two Fridays out of four. Tom Slater was always coming out from behind the bar. He and Stuart Sharf loved to protect Sam, who, because of his sharp tongue, usually needed it. One day, Sam was just sitting at Table 18 talking with Stan Delaplane when this guy, who, I guess, Sam had insulted in some way, walked over and dumped an entire bottle of wine on him. Sam, bless him, didn't blink an eye. At first he looked as if nothing had happened at all. Then, very slowly, he got up and said, 'Sir, I hope you've had a wonderful time because this is the last one you'll ever have here.' And he had Slater escort the guy out of there. I always enjoyed Slater, but he was the real king of the abusers. I used to tell him, 'Tom, everybody is entitled to one or two vices, but you've got them all: women, booze, drugs, and gambling.' And I think gambling was his worst addiction. If he had a bad day at the track, it was tough getting a drink out of him.

"It was so seductive working here, so much like a family. There was no racial or religious prejudice. When one of the Chinese busboys got married, we all went, and he hired an interpreter for us so we'd know what was going on in the ceremony. And we loved Peter Yeung. I firmly believe that Korean girlfriend he had did him in. He got wild and crazy when he was around that gold digger. I'm sure she got him in all that gambling trouble.

"I left here February 6, 1984, eight years to the day after I was hired. My reasons? Oh I don't know. I guess I didn't think I was getting enough respect. Ed, you know, has this sneaking suspicion that women are really more competent than men, and he resents them for it. And then he'd start sending memos addressed to 'tipped employees,' and I never liked being called a 'tipped employee.' So one day, I took Sam aside and over a little White Label and soda, I told him it was time for me to leave. My personal philosophy is that you should never leave a place angry because if you do you won't really have left it at all. I really loved it here, and I'll never forget it. It was an important segment of my life, a postgraduate school where I learned a lot. And I think I gave a lot. I guess one reason I left was to find out if there really was a life after the Washington Square Bar & Grill. And the funny thing is, for a long time there really wasn't."

Mark is alone at the table, but there is a full plate of pasta, a place serving, and a glass of cabernet opposite him on the table. Moose had been there only moments before, but something presumably pressing had called him away from the table. Mark eats alone, blissfully oblivious to his luncheon partner's defection. He is aware, however, that we are watching him, so he makes an elaborate business of talking to the empty chair before him. There is much laughter as the conversation with the invisible seatmate becomes much more animated. Finally, Sullivan calls out, "Mark, just exactly who are you having lunch with?" Mark looks up, as if startled by the interruption. "Chris," he replies, "I'd like you to meet my friend, Harvey."

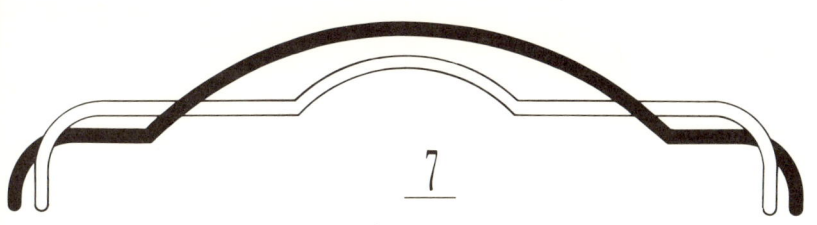

7

The New Wave

The character of a saloon will change as subtly as a person's. This is particularly true of a saloon like The Square, which is no more than the sum of the multifarious personalities who work and play there. In the broadest sense, it may be said that Ed Moose gives the place its energy and strength, Sam Deitsch its jazzy soul, and Mary Etta its heart. And the steadying presence of Mark Schachern gives it what stability it can muster. But these are merely the obvious sources of The Square's persona. The daily ebb and flow of life there gives it a constantly changing face. And there is no question that as it has gotten older, it has taken on a somewhat more subdued aspect. Indeed, the raffish sorts who originally peopled the place on one side of the bar or the other have pretty well passed on. The Square is still a noisy joint, but deep down in its heart of hearts, it is much quieter.

More than anyone else, Schachern is responsible for this relative serenity. An ex-schoolteacher, he was hired more or less to bring the class to order. But he's not by any definition a prude. As the son of a veteran Detroit newspaperman, he learned early about the underside of life. He can drink with the best of them, and he has a tart self-deprecating sense of humor. At the same time, he is a loyal father and husband, and his dedication to his job even astonishes his partners. Mark had worked at a number of San Francisco bars and restaurants, part of the time to supplement his bare-bones income as a schoolteacher, before he came to The Square as a waiter in March 1979. He was just thirty years old, but he had a broad range of experience in the business, from waiting tables and pouring drinks to managing accounts.

But Moose was less impressed with these credentials than with his prowess as a softball player. Mark also profited from some inside influence. His wife, Jan, had worked there as a waitress, and bartender Riofski, a fellow USF alumnus, was an old friend from the days when both worked at Pat O'Shea's bar. But it wasn't until Mark began spraying the North Beach playground with line drives that Moose, the frustrated Durocher, decided he'd make an excellent waiter. And Mark did prove to be a superior employee, so good at his job that when Hal Thunes finally concluded he'd reached burnout, Mark replaced him at the door. He had been working there barely three months.

The Square was now approaching a turning point in its brief lifetime. The madcap days were winding down, and the place was starting to do some serious business. Thunes, smooth-talking and street-wise, had been invaluable when life in the saloon was more freewheeling. The new prosperity called for a steadier hand in control of the staff. Mark seemed to Ed and Sam to be as steady as they came. He was appointed manager of the place, and within a year he became a partner, on $50,000 he borrowed from Sam.

When he first took charge, Mark saw only chaos. "There was no real organization at all," he recalls. "The place was a lot of fun, but the food was mediocre and there were no controls over the staff. By ten o'clock at night, the bartenders were all shit-faced and just having a good time talking to each other. Slater and Hal used to play cards all day back then, and there were times when they'd come in pretty screwed up. For that matter, the whole staff was all screwed up. I was frankly agog. It was obvious we weren't doing as well as we could be doing. It had been fun for five years, but by now the place was starting to take off. It was time to get down to business and make this thing work."

Suddenly, the division of labor, only vaguely defined before, became somewhat clearer. Mark was in charge of hiring and firing on the floor and he would supervise purchasing at the bar, then nominally managed by a hot-tempered Irishman, Cyril Boyce. Mary Etta would oversee the kitchen and decide what should appear on the menu. Sam, the fussiest and most experienced of the bunch, the compulsive emptier of ashtrays, would be the floorwalker. Ed would be the boniface, the PR man, the guy out front.

"The place was really starting to roll," says Mark. "It was an exciting time. We were all working hard and enjoying ourselves. It was truly amazing the way Ed worked this town. Everybody seemed to know him. This became *the* labor hangout. The plumbers, the longshoremen, they all came here. The Square was really becoming famous. People were beginning to realize they could walk in here and know they'd have a good time."

But then some "weeding out" was needed. "There was heavy drinking and even some drugs going on with the staff," says Mark. "Drinking may be a part of this business, but there was need for some control. Ed and Sam had made a commitment to run a first-class operation."

In place of the Rudy Runamoks and pistol-packing bartenders, most of whom had gone their own unsteady way by the time The Square made the turn to the straight and narrow, Mark hired "younger, more energetic people," waiters and waitresses such as Rick Snyder, Marcy Campagne, and Arlene Cieply-soon-to-be-Boyle. Still there were unseemly episodes. Cyril and Ed got into a shouting match at the bar one late afternoon when Ed remarked to his bar manager that the men's room was short of towels and Cyril replied crisply that the bathroom was hardly under his jurisdiction. It was an argument Cyril could not win, so after a succession of remarks Ed considered impertinent, he was noisily cashiered. Maître d' Clancy and bartender Yee were also sent packing after a drink-induced after-hours altercation was taken onto the street with sorry consequences for the older, smaller Yee. Clancy was a briskly efficient maître d', capable of both mollifying and eventually seating overflow dinner crowds. But he was also a far too active street fighter — "a thug," says Riofski; "self destructive," says Mark. Yee was in the original Square mold, an off-the-wall sort who in those robust times liked his booze both on and off the job. Ordinarily cheerful, even in his cups, Yee became riled by Clancy's taunts on the fateful night and, feeling that his manhood was at stake, accepted the younger man's invitation to step outside. Defending his manhood cost him a black eye and, ultimately, his job.

Finding a replacement for the talented Clancy was a daunting task. Ed and Sam hadn't required much in the way of professional expertise from Clancy's predecessors, some of whom were rank amateurs, like Tom Shess, a magazine editor who filled in at the door for a few weeks with disastrous results, once overbooking the dining room by fifty reservations. The maître d' problem was finally resolved with the hiring of Dick Broderick, who came highly recommended after working for years at the then-legendary no-name bar run by Neil Davis in Sausalito. Mark pretty much had the staff he wanted when the summer of 1984 and its twelve-thousand-dollar nights came along. In place of the wild hares of old, he had speedy, smart, and unflappable young waiters and waitresses at the ready. And he was a benevolent boss, a morale booster, a confidant, even a playmate, for he was really just one of the gang, despite his position. It was a happy staff. The people who worked there spent their days off together, had parties together, even took vacations together. They were having such a good time that hardly anyone even thought of leaving The Square. Restaurant employees mostly live a vagabond life, bounding from job to job as the mood seizes them. Square employees were the exception. They were in for the duration. And why not? The money was good, with tips as much as six hundred dollars a week for a waiter or waitress, and work was where your pals were.

Arlene Boyle and Marcy Campagne started work there only two months apart in 1980. It's been the time of their lives. "I love my job," says Marcy. "We all do. Even when I'm on vacation, I love to come back to work. I love to shuck and jive with the customers. I guess you can say I'm annotating their dining experience. Hell, I feed these guys more often than their wives do. And I want people at my tables to enjoy themselves. That's easy enough because I'm enjoying myself. I think of The Square as unique in that sense. The atmosphere is so relaxed. You might say the curtain of formality is dropped here."

Arlene and Marcy are beautiful women in their thirties. Marcy is tall, blond, and blue-eyed; Arlene is prematurely gray but with a young face and arresting violet eyes. Beauty notwithstanding, both women are not above showing up for work in outlandish and unflattering costumes. On Halloween 1987, for example, they came as Jim and Tammy Bakker and went trick-or-treating across the street at Little City. Marcy has also appeared as Los Angeles Lakers player Kurt Rambis, as wrestler Hulk Hogan, and, on one red-letter day, as Vanna White. Marcy is so flashy and outgoing that Moose once told her she was too noisy to make a good bartender. Arlene is quieter, but equally assertive. When she first fell in love with Mike Boyle, an old friend of Mark's, she contrived to switch stations with other waiters so she would always serve him. The ploy worked. Within a few months Mike asked her to marry him.

Marcy and Arlene are the last two waitresses The Square has hired, but when they first came to work there, they had plenty of female company. Sofi was in her prime then, "a flat-out star," says Arlene. And there was Dianne Mansfield, cute and plump, an archaeologist who was married briefly to Tom Slater. And Judy Berkley, a Joan Blondell in Square black, a wisecracker, tough and witty, yet vulnerable. Judy was a freelance writer, and she and Sofi collaborated on a sardonic but actually quite informative guide for unattached women in San Francisco, entitled *Single File*. The book was based in large part on their own experiences and supplemented with extensive interviews they had with available men, most of them Square customers. Sofi's experiences as a psychiatric social worker came into useful play here, so she did the bulk of the interviewing. Judy added a fine touch to the prose. She also wrote an irreverent piece on life in The Square for *San Francisco* magazine, which the editors entitled "Secrets of the Washbag."

Even if the ramshackle premises could be duplicated and the mania extrapolated, there's only one each of Moose and Deitsch. There's no replicating these unique personalities. Physically and temperamentally, the partners are miles apart, but The Square's whacky human drama gets its imprimatur from both these eccentric saloon Diaghilevs.

Onstage, Moose is a model of warmth and charm. When he sets out to captivate, few can resist being sucked in. Lillian Hellman, however, eluded his viscous blandishments. Spotting the literary grand dame at a window table, Moose oozed over to perform the Rite of Extreme Unctuousness. "Ms. Hellman," he said, "I'm sorry it's so noisy and smoky in here today." The chain-smoking writer, who had a face like an alligator handbag, shot Moose a reptillian look through a curtain of smoke, croaking, "I *like* noisy, smoky bars."

While Moose attends to the high-visibility aspects of running The Square, Deitsch directs the staff with management-training techniques lifted from the Book of Job. His obsessive attention to details — straightening pictures, flicking imperceptible motes of dust, and precisely aligning ashtrays — has given rise to a theory among family members that Deitsch is pioneering a new field of science: ashtray physics.

When Sofi left, Judy became the ranking Square waitress. She was also easily the most influential. Her serious involvement with the union and her steadfast refusal to take her bosses seriously made her something of an irritant to Ed and Sam. Mark was the buffer, keeping both sides apart. The women at The Square also had reason to be grateful to Mark for his then-unorthodox practice of hiring relatively sane male co-workers, a departure from Ed's, in their opinion, ruinous policy of employing only certifiable lunatics. Gone were the raving blouse-rippers of old, replaced by waiters more interested in performance than in terrorizing the ladies. "Those other guys just didn't function," says Arlene. "At least not for long."

The sane men were more fun, too. And life on the floor at The Square seemed at times like one big game show. Judy identified customers by their habitual orders: "Here comes Shrimp Louie and Mrs. Cheeseburger." Arlene and Marcy kept everyone alert with the game Impressions: "If you were weather what would you be?" And Gary Epting had his massive collection of memorable names culled from customers' credit cards: Lucky Pantages, Donald J. Angst, Richard Robbins Pancake, Maureen A. Footlick, Fatima Brazil, Roger P. Tubby, Bonsal Glasscake, Emily S. Fudge, Pecos Bill Field. Even on the slowest nights, there were few dull moments backstage at The Square.

But for all the hokum, the place was run with astonishing professionalism. Judy Berkley had already left to get married when *San Francisco* magazine came out in January 1987 with a poll ranking waiters and bartenders in town. The Square easily dominated the list. Bobby Ryder and Bill Oates were rated as two of the top four waiters in town, Marcy and alumna Sofi were among the four best waitresses, and Dennis O'Connor was deservedly listed as one of the eight best bartenders. The poll also reflected the amazing diversity of The Square's staff. Bobby Ryder and Bill Oates, for example, could not be more different in appearance and style. Oates is a tall and handsome black man, so suave he'd make Bobby Short look like a mendicant. He knows his customers so well he routinely writes down their orders before they give them, and he's right fully ninety percent of the time. Bobby Ryder is a tiny (five-foot-two, barely a hundred pounds) nervous and nervy ex–New Yorker. In his relatively brief stay at The Square (he left in July 1988 after only four years), he became one of the most popular and sought-after waiters in the joint. In fact, Bobby didn't so much serve his customers as join them. It was not at all uncommon for him to pull up a chair at a table full of regulars and entertain them with the latest developments in his domestic travails, the antics of his young son Tyler, or, if he was really in an expansive humor, the status of his own wildly fluctuating sex life. According to Gary Epting's diagnosis, waiters guilty of excessive sociability suffer from the "Bobby Ryder Syndrome."

Bobby had a million of 'em. "Have you ever seen this one?" he might inquire of a startled patron as he snatched the edge of the tablecloth and feigned jerking it out from under the dishes, glasses, and silverware. "An excellent choice, sir," he would obsequiously commend a customer who had ordered nothing more inspiring than a cheeseburger. Or, taking mock offense at some imagined slight, he might gather up a patron's place setting with angry swiftness and march off with it, only to return seconds later grinning satanically. "What the hell," Bobby would say, "some of these assholes will only be here an hour or so. Why not have a good time?"

But it was not all laughs for the little man. He suffered through a long and emotionally draining divorce and custody battle, and when he finally won the right to keep his six-year-old son, he decided to move with him to the comparative serenity of Portland, Oregon. On his last night on the job, his fellow waiters and waitresses playfully ripped his tiny tuxedo to shreds before throwing him a huge going-away party. Bobby was moved to tears. "This was the best restaurant job I've ever had," he said before he departed for the north woods. "There was a great chemistry at The Square. They encourage you to have a personality. My first year, we had the All-Star game and the convention, and I couldn't believe the business. That was the most amazing run I've ever seen any place have. And the way the people in the kitchen handled it! I've never seen a better kitchen. They're sweethearts in there. It seems like there's always something going on at The Square. I like the high visibility you'd get there. I was proud to tell people I worked there. It's funny, the place looks like crap, but everybody in there looks good. Maybe that's because they're having fun. There's no place like it. It reeks of New York and could just as well be in the Village, but it's perfect for San Francisco.

"But I'm not afraid of giving the whole thing up. The important thing is I'm on an even keel now, so I can handle changes. My two years of paying alimony are over, and I've got custody of my boy. I also know I can't wait tables for the next twenty years. Hell, I'm a bright guy, and I know there's something else waiting for me out there. You know, when

I was a little kid, I ran a lot. Whenever anything went wrong, I'd start running. If I didn't do well in school, I'd just run somewhere. Well, the running's over now. I can walk away from here with a smile on my face."

Bobby, who has been a waiter for most of his adult life, wants out of the business. At least three of his colleagues on the floor, all of whom have had other and more challenging occupations, see waiting tables as a career. Gary Epting is a successful painter, Rick Snyder is a cabinetmaker, and Jim Gallup had studied to be an anthropologist. All are now committed to The Square. Snyder has been there since 1979 and Epting and Gallup since 1982. Working there has been a sort of reunion for them. All three grew up in Traverse City, Michigan, and went to Western Michigan University. Their bosses call them, and with good cause, the Michigan Fraternity. When Mark called Epting and Gallup about joining their old pal Snyder on the floor, Epting sounded a note of apprehension. "You know, Mark," he said, "Jim and I aren't characters. We're just competent." "That," replied Mark, "is exactly what we're looking for." And it's just what they got, for these three approach their work with uncommon seriousness.

"So many people are not content with being just a waiter," says Gallup. "People in this business tend to dwell in a kind of fantasy world, to live a lifestyle they can't support. Think about it. A waiter will walk away from work every night with sixty or seventy fresh dollars in his pocket. That can give you a real sense of power. If you're not disciplined, all the money can go as quickly as it came, particularly on drugs. But I see this as my job. It's what I plan on doing. I like it. I enjoy the challenge of a busy evening. I feel like an air traffic controller on those nights. Every waiter has his own style. Mine is to maintain a distance. I think people who insist you should always be smiling for them don't belong in the Washington Square Bar & Grill."

"Right," says Epting. "I'm not your clown for the evening. Nobody should expect me to sing "Happy Birthday" for them. But I will be sensitive to my customers' needs. I will serve Scott Beach maybe four or five times a week. I can tell when things are going well for him, when he has work. In time, you get to know the habits of the regular customers, to recognize their ups and downs. I love to see the same people come in every day the way they do for lunch. You develop a relationship."

"It's like old home week in there," says Snyder. "It's one of the reasons I love my job. I think it's my responsibility to communicate that love, that strong feeling for the place, to the customers. You must learn to treat your customers as individuals. Some you can banter with. Some you commiserate with. I see them on the way up and on the way down. I feel a sense of participation in their lives."

"I do not look at my job as demeaning in any way," says Gallup. "I think a lot of creativity goes into it. The idea is to give the illusion, even when you're at your busiest, that it's all so easy. On a magic night when all the right people are in the right place, it's a little like seeing a good play."

"A night in a restaurant is just a little piece of time," says Epting. "There is a flow to it. And yet the waiters are really the only ones moving around. We are the migratory ones. We move as if in a hive. Or you could say we're the racehorses constantly on the go, the thoroughbreds."

Hank Greenwald, the baseball announcer, is having lunch in the main dining room. For months there have been rumors, since confirmed, that Hank would leave the Yankee broadcasts and return to the Giants, where he belongs. He was a popular guy here, a sharp baseball observer but with enough understated wit to take the edge off. Got in a beef with the station manager and hustled off to New York for the big bucks. But New Yorkers like their broadcasters aggressive and opinionated. San Franciscans prefer them funny. Then there's the Steinbrenner factor. Nobody lasts long with George. And it's been common knowledge for months that Hank wants to come back home. Better check to see how he's doing.

"Hey, Hank, how long you gonna be in town?"

"Well, I'm usually around as long as the Yankees are."

"So, how's it going?"

"What can I say?"

"And how're you getting along with George?"

"Let's put it this way: I call him Mr. Steinbrenner. And he calls me Big Fella. Then he asks somebody next to him who the hell I am."

Hank will be back.

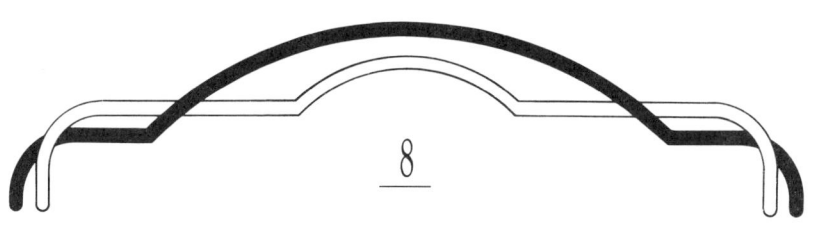

8

Splendid! What's Softball?

Not many years had passed in the life of The Square before it became known as Ed Moose's place. The big man had finally found his calling as a restaurateur, and if it was Dorenbush who coaxed the right people into the joint, it was Moose who kept them there. He was the perfect host, an indefatigable table-hopper, and a quick study in the art of celebrity greasing. And in time, he became something of a celebrity himself. His friend from the ill-fated Harris presidential campaign, investment banker Herbert Allen, had much to do with this. Allen, the money man, had important ties to both politics and show business. He was that rarest of Wall Streeters, a Democrat, intimate with the likes of Walter Mondale and Senator Bill Bradley. He was pals also with such journalists and writers as Tom Brokaw and Tom Wolfe. And because his firm, Allen & Company, had bought controlling interest of Columbia Pictures in 1973 (since sold), he quickly became an important figure in Hollywood. As Moose's friendship with this dashing financier solidified, the kid from Holy Name Parish found himself speeding dizzily ahead in the fast lane.

The Moose-Allen friendship, unlikely as it appeared on the surface, was in fact mutually rewarding. Allen was a notorious risk-taker, both as a financier and a movie magnate. But in his private life he was much less a playboy than a rigidly well organized, early-to-bed, early-to-rise, basically nondrinking health fanatic. Moose, the volatile, hard-drinking

Irishman from the wrong side of the tracks, both entertained him and provided him with a fresh perspective. Moose was unlike anyone else Allen had met in his world of privilege and power.

And Ed was equally enamored of his rich friend. Power of any sort had always held him in thrall, and Allen had it to burn in several worlds. At the same time, Herb could be fun. He was quick-witted and he liked nothing better than an afternoon of playing softball, and this game became Moose's enduring passion and, curiously enough, a prime source of both his and his restaurant's gathering popularity. Allen's important friends were, for their part, charmed by the man from San Francisco. Moose would see them on his spur-of-the-moment trips to Hollywood or in New York, where Ed stayed with Herb at the Allen apartment in the Carlyle Hotel, or at the Allen estate in Southampton, or at political seminars in Sun Valley. And somehow, these big shots all found their way back to the Washington Square Bar & Grill. Overnight, it seemed, The Square had been transformed from a neighborhood bar to a place where the elite meet to eat.

As his fortunes increased, Moose began to travel more. Rome was one of his regular stops and so was Paris, where he soon developed friendships with vintners and restaurateurs. He grew particularly friendly with a young Englishman named Steve Spurrier, who was an internationally respected wine connoisseur and the part-owner of a Paris restaurant near Maxim's called Le Moulin du Village. Spurrier had become a frequent visitor to the Napa Valley wine country north of San Francisco and, because of his friendship with Moose, a regular on these visits at The Square, where he and Ed would enjoy long and vinous lunches together. And when Moose was in Paris, he unfailingly stopped in at Le Moulin. It was at one of these Moulin meetings in October 1978 that Spurrier, growing sentimental, suggested that the two restaurants engage in some sort of forks-across-the-sea exchange. What could they do, he asked Moose, to bring the staff and customers of each place together on common ground? Moose pondered this for a moment and then was seized with inspiration. "Why don't we play softball?" he blurted out. "Splendid!" replied Spurrier enthusiastically. "What's softball?"

Le Moulin, quite naturally, had no team. But there were some on the staff, Americans mostly, who unlike Spurrier had at least heard of the game. The Square had had a team of sorts for several years, one hastily assembled by Moose for an annual game with Cookie Picetti's Star Buffet at the North Beach playground's asphalt diamond. Cookie's team was composed mostly of burly cops who could hit the ball a mile. They regularly trounced The Square's random assortment of waiters, bartenders, and hungover customers. The early losses did not sit well with Moose, whose competitiveness passes beyond the merely fierce to the very perimeters of psychosis. So he began actively recruiting better athletes, although giving lip service at least to his dictum, agreed upon by his original team, that all of his players must be over forty years of age or have medical proof of liver malfunction. By 1978, his team had achieved a near competitive balance with Cookie's cops. Claude Jarman, the former child movie star who won a special Oscar for *The Yearling* in 1946, was then as now a successful San Francisco businessman. He was also Moose's shortstop, a right-handed hitter with power. Jerry McGrath, a stockbroker, was a speedy leadoff man. Jimmy Igoe, a lawyer, was a slick infielder and a good left-handed hitter. And Chris Sullivan, who had been a Cookie's regular, agreed to make the jump to Moose's team. Moose was the pitcher and fiery manager. "He makes Durocher look like Jean Hersholt," one of The Square's players said of him. As Moose's power over his players grew, his employees prudently dropped off the team one by one, preferring to confine their contact with the boss to the restaurant itself, where his tantrums were less frequent and not so easily provoked.

Spurrier was unaware of Moose's increasingly meticulous preparations. The Englishman, of course, wouldn't have recognized a good team if he'd seen one. He was content to round up what few persons he knew who could tell a softball from a grapefruit. The preliminary plans for the international game were made in secret by Moose and Spurrier. Then in the winter of 1978, Moose began informing his players (one of them the author) that the schedule would be twice as long that year. We would play Cookie's, as usual, and then on Mother's Day, we would travel to the Bois de Boulogne to play Le Moulin du Village. We would, that is, if the players could afford the trip, The Square's team budget being limited to the purchase of our uniforms (white T-shirts emblazoned with the restaurant's logo). Jarman, who was then a partner in a travel agency, would provide discounts on airfares and hotel accommodations. Still, Paris is not renowned as a cheap vacation spot, and Moose was fearful his players, many of them rather noisily on the shorts, would not come up with the ready. He approached George Yee, one of his bartenders, first. Yee did not hesitate: he peeled off two hundred dollars and said, "This is a down payment. Count me in." In no time, the manager had more than thirty volunteers, nearly half of them single women in The Square's formidable real-estate luncheon brigade.

No one knew it at the time, but the Paris game would be the first in a series. From that point on, Moose would strive to schedule a road game on exotic soil, and whenever possible, on Mother's Day, his reasoning being that anyone young enough to have a living mother did not belong on his team (this, despite the fact that his own mother was very much alive). The Paris trip would also give the team its distinctive nickname. On the transatlantic flight, several of the supposedly bilingual team members began hacking about for a name that would capture, on the one hand, the Gallic flavor of the experience and, on the other, some sense of the madcap nature of the players. In English, it was concluded, we would be called Wild Hares. This was confidently translated to *Les Lapins Sauvages* in French. We thus became, in our ignorance then and forever, The Washington Square Bar & Grill Wild Rabbits. We decided never to retranslate ourselves back into English, so "Les Lapins Sauvages" we have remained.

The game itself was, regrettably but unavoidably, a comedy of errors. There was little chance it could have been much else, considering our opponents' unfamiliarity with the sport (several of their players put gloves on their *throwing* hands) and the site of the game, a rutted and rocky soccer field in the Bois. Moose's normally scrupulous attention to detail failed him embarrassingly in this regard, for he must have entertained some romantic notion that every stretch of lawn in the Bois had the texture of a putting green. In reality, there was scarcely five square feet anywhere that did not look as if it had been a battlefield. As a result, such elementary skills as fielding ground balls became adventures in dangerous living. Our infielders were more concerned, and rightly so, with protecting their private parts from potentially crippling bad hops than with making the routine plays. Our first baseman, Steve Strauss, had only two putouts, one of them at home plate, in the course of a desultory four-inning, two-hour game. If anything, our skills deteriorated in every inning, partly because of an increasing awareness of the hazardous field conditions — there was a yawning ditch not three feet from third base — but mostly on account of the appearance in the very first inning of a case of Piper Heidseck champagne on the sidelines. While the bubbly seemed to play havoc with the rest of us, it proved a restorative for Yee, who was unable to start the game at second base because of an apparently terminal hangover. But after several long pulls of Piper Heidseck he announced himself fit to play and, in fact, conducted himself in championship form in the single inning he saw action.

The outfielders had it relatively easy, since fly balls were not affected by the appalling field conditions, as infield grounders consistently were. If an outfielder could avoid stumbling into a trench, he had a chance, denied to the infielders, of preserving his dignity. Allen, who flew in from New York for the game, as he would for all subsequent games, was declared by Moose to be our Most Valuable Player. There may have been some favoritism involved in this selection, but in all fairness, Allen did have a good day, going five-for-five at the plate and making all the plays in center field. It was the start of a big week for the financier, apart from the millions he routinely accumulated in his place of business. Not three days after our game, he apprehended a fleeing armed robber on Madison Avenue and was hailed as a hero in the New York press, including the *Times*. Moose was disappointed in reading these accounts to discover that there was no mention of his MVP performance in Paris.

The Paris game gave Europeans a chance to see the Moose softball mania close at hand. The restaurateur was the soul of diplomacy and cosmopolitan charm in all of his off-field dealings with the Moulin contingent. But once the game began, he became the raving lunatic we had come to know. "He's a little like the mean little kid who keeps saying, 'It's my ball so you have to do what I say,' " said Sullivan in an apt description. The Moulin crowd could not believe they were seeing the same man. We could. When ground balls began caroming off our chests and foreheads and rolling unimpeded between our legs, Moose cried out in real pain, "Can't anybody here play this game?" It's a familiar lament, first uttered by Casey Stengel when he managed the hapless '62 Mets, but Moose seemed so genuinely anguished he sent a shiver through us. And when Jarman threw a ball five feet over Strauss's head after actually fielding a ground ball, Moose summarily banished him to short center and brought in the versatile Sullivan to play shortstop. It was a decision that rankled Jarman and one that would have dire physical consequences for Igoe, then playing second base. Later that same long inning, Sullivan and Igoe collided in pursuit of a pop-up, and since the police officer outweighed the lawyer by a good sixty pounds, it was Igoe, already drowsy with wine, who fell to the dirt unconscious. He was soon revived, however, and with Moose fuming, the game resumed.

But Moose saved his most unseemly display for late in the game, when Spurrier attempted to replace some of his inexperienced Frenchmen with a few marines, on duty at the American Embassy, who showed up to take in the fun. Moose was apoplectic. "No one plays who's under forty," he bellowed. The oldest marine was perhaps twenty-four. This was a rule, loosely applied to our own team, that Spurrier, enjoying (he thought) an amusing romp, was unaware of until Moose's outburst. Finally, after much stomping about and cursing by our manager (Sullivan was now calling him the Ugly American), a compromise was reached: one marine, a muscular black youth of about twenty-two, could play for Le Moulin. As it developed, he wasn't much better than the weary Frenchman he replaced, although at third base I blanched in expectation of his rocketing an unplayable and probably physically debilitating ground ball right at me. The leatherneck popped up instead to end the game. The final score was either 40–22, or 42–20, in our favor. That's a lot of scoring for four innings, but Moose was not pleased with our performance.

He was hardly displeased, however, with the publicity this otherwise forgettable game generated. Four journalists had made the trip from San Francisco, so Moose had every reason to expect some ink afterward. He was staggered by the final outpouring. Both San Francisco newspapers, the *Chronicle* and the *Examiner*, ran lengthy feature stories. And *Sports Illustrated* ran some seven thousand words, complete with illustrations. The Square was just beginning to be known as *the* spot to be in San Francisco; now it was becoming famous nationwide. Moose was receiving challenges from bar owners all over the country, and he became a talk-show regular from San Diego to Portland, Maine. Wisely, he rejected all the various challenges as being unworthy. Besides, he had his own agenda for our team, an agenda ordered to take every advantage of this first rush of publicity. Les Lapins Sauvages would only go where the action was.

In 1980, the team traveled to New York to defeat *Sports Illustrated*

16–3 in a game played in the rain at Central Park. Moose advertised the game in the *New York Times*, and a bellboy, summoned by our manager from the Mayflower Hotel to replenish the beer supply, had a time at bat for Les Lapins. He singled, but when he returned to the hotel in a mud-caked uniform, he was fired on the spot. Moose agreed to hire him if he ever made it to San Francisco.

The next year, with much fanfare, Moose took the team for a tour of England and Ireland. Moose and Dorenbush telephoned regular reports on our progress back to Bay Area radio stations. Fans of the Jim Dunbar talk show were especially well-informed, partly because Dunbar had become a Square regular himself and partly because he had been a classmate of Dorenbush's at Michigan State. There was, however, little to report, since for once Moose was unable to schedule a game. Instead, practices were held on a rugby pitch at Oxford and on a sheep pasture outside Blenheim Palace. "We are having difficulty finding opponents," one radio report back to Dunbar began, "so we are playing with ourselves."

In 1982, Les Lapins played the Rutherford Vineyards in the Napa Valley wine country. And in 1983, the team played in Hollywood (actually, nearby Encino) against a Columbia Pictures squad organized in part by Herb Allen and producer Ray Stark and featuring an array of leggy starlets. Allen, ever loyal to Moose, played for Les Lapins against his own film studio. And Moose, despite his reverence for the movie crowd, became embroiled in two major disputes, one before the game over the Columbia team's footwear (some of their players were wearing spikes) and one during the game over the unpaid umpire's ball and strike calls behind the plate. The unfortunate arbiter had come to the ballpark in a lighthearted mood, expecting the game to be nothing more than a carefree outing. He was understandably stunned when confronted by an apparent madman and had to be placated later by Sullivan, pitching in relief of Moose.

The Square reached perhaps the zenith of its popularity at the time of the 1984 Democratic National Convention in San Francisco. The place was packed solid from noon to midnight and beyond. The crowds became so dense, in fact, that Sam and Ed had to hire security guards to keep customers *out*, an action that did not sit at all well with some late-arriving regulars. Among the customers that memorable week were most of the major candidates, including Walter Mondale, and all of the television luminaries, including the three network anchormen: Brokaw, Peter Jennings, and Dan Rather. Crowds both outside and in the joint would applaud as the celebrities debouched from their limos. The biggest responses of all, according to bartender Riofski's unofficial applause meter, were accorded television's elder statesman, Walter Cronkite. The week before the convention, *Time* magazine had put The Square on its map of important places to see in San Francisco. Moose was ecstatic, and he used the occasion to schedule a game at the North Beach playground with a media team captained by Brokaw and featuring Bryant Gumbel, Jennings, Jeff Greenfield, and New York Governor Mario Cuomo. Cuomo, the convention's keynote speaker, actually played for both sides, grounding out for the media team and singling home a run for the winning Lapins side. An account of the game, complete with photos of the governor, appeared in *People* magazine.

Brokaw insisted on a rematch the following year in New York. The game was played on a field near Allen's estate in Southampton, thereby minimizing the New York team's home field advantage, but Les Lapins lost 14–9 anyway. It was the team's first defeat in the road series, and Moose was devastated. He blamed the loss on two factors: the illegal fast-pitching of the media team's Mort Zuckerman, a financier and publisher, and his own foolish decision to serve champagne on the bus transporting the team from midtown Manhattan to the Hamptons, a drive long enough to leave many of his key players at less than peak efficiency.

But not even this loss, embarrassing as it was, could stem the manager's mounting ambitions for his softball program, and his plans grew ever more grandiose. Boston Mayor Raymond Flynn, of all people, would eventually lead him in a new direction. Flynn had become a Square regular on his trips west. And his was a positive influence in more ways than one. Inordinately fond of the Irish singing group the Clancy Brothers, he would deliver renditions of treasured ballads late into the evening with such accompanists as Riofski and the then *San Francisco Examiner* editor David Burgin. His performances occasionally lasted beyond the 2:00 A.M. closing hour, an oversight the beat cops brought gently but forcefully to Moose's attention. Flynn's enthusiasm for the San Francisco saloon was such that, like Spurrier before him, he suggested the crowd there should come on back to Boston. Why not, he suggested, play a softball game at Fenway Park? The Red Sox, he noted, would be out of town on Mother's Day, and he would be willing to make all the necessary arrangements. Moose, envisioning yet another publicity binge for Les Lapins, happily agreed.

Fenway Park is one of baseball's three oldest ballparks and probably its most beloved. Comiskey Park in Chicago, which was built in 1911, a year earlier than Fenway, is the oldest, but it is a decaying and unloved wreck. Fenway's only true rival for the affections of baseball purists is Chicago's other park, Wrigley Field, which opened for business in 1914. The seed of something big began to hatch in Moose's fevered brain. Quick research revealed to him that no team in the history of baseball, or certainly softball, had ever played games in these two cherished stadiums on successive days. What if games could be arranged for Les Lapins in Fenway on Mother's Day and in Wrigley the next day? Exercising his clout with the media, Moose was able to enlist the aid of Andrew McKenna of the *Chicago Tribune* family, and a member of the Cubs' board of directors, in setting up the second game. What a coup! Les Lapins against Flynn's All Stars on Mother's Day and then, twenty-four hours later, against whatever team the Chicago media could slap together.

Now Moose felt he had to light a fire under the players who had disgraced themselves in Southampton. He began composing urgent memos to team members, warning them that in these two hallowed ballparks they could expect to face teams of near major league caliber. Brokaw, he was certain, would bring in "ringers." Actually, the Southampton game was an aberration, a calamity brought on partly by overindulgence on the bus trip. Moose had, since the Paris fiasco, steadily improved his team to the point where it could hold its own in most slow-pitch softball leagues. Where once he had fielded a squad of true Square regulars, middle-aged guys who would rather talk baseball than play it, now he had younger and better athletes, some with college or even professional experience. He had also added some experienced women players then active in various Bay Area leagues. It had become increasingly difficult for Moose's original players, none of whom was getting either younger or better, to break into the lineup. And some, notably Jarman and Igoe, just dropped out. Moose's almost pathologic dread of losing had driven him far afield from the old "wild rabbit" philosophy. His newer players were not much, if at all, over forty, and there was not a bad liver in the lot. He had no trouble at all recruiting talent, particularly from among the legal community, where it was recognized that a reasonably coordinated lawyer could get himself some valuable free publicity in a Lapins uniform.

There was, however, one newer player who represented a significant departure from the youth-and-fitness movement. Herb Caen had long been a baseball enthusiast and had, in fact, played some serious amateur ball in his younger days in his hometown of Sacramento and his adopted (since 1936) city of San Francisco. He first played for Moose in the 1984 Democratic Convention game, and though he was sent sprawling there in a collision at first base, he decided to sign on as a Lapin. He was seventy years old in 1986, but he still entertained boyish delusions about his skills as a first sacker. In truth, he could catch any ball thrown or hit directly to him with the old-time grace, but his running and throwing betrayed him as a septuagenarian. Caen bought a new mitt for the Fenway-Wrigley doubleheader ("It will take ten years to break it in, and I don't have that long"), and he outfitted himself for the games in a full-dress red-and-white uniform. He was a happy addition to the thirty-player traveling squad to Boston and Chicago, and he particularly made glad the heart of his manager by devoting three full-length columns to the occasion.

Moose worked mightily to prepare us physically and mentally for two more supposedly invincible foes. In his pregame speeches in both Boston and Chicago he reminded us solemnly that the honor of San Francisco was at stake in these games. But even before stage and movie star Ann Reinking sang the National Anthem for us in Boston, we could see once again that we were playing a casually assembled team of happy-go-lucky old guys who had swallowed whole Moose's portrayal of Les Lapins as hapless tosspots. Our opponents, in fact, were astonished to see us trot onto the consecrated Fenway turf in brand-new red warm-up jackets. They, a number that included detective novelist Bob Parker and *Boston Globe* editorial page editor Marty Nolan, were dressed as if for a Sunday-afternoon picnic. We beat them 10-4 and immediately enplaned for Chicago for the second half of the doubleheader, a privileged few making their way in Allen's private jet.

An even more disorganized team confronted us at Wrigley. In fact, only minutes before the Reinking national anthem, it was one player short. We won 21-5. But even when we were ahead by something like 15-0, Moose began to fret over our increasingly casual play. "Don't let up out there," he cautioned. "What's the matter with you guys?" Moose was even more out of sorts than usual, if that is possible, because his own active participation in these games was curtailed by a torn left biceps, an injury suffered in one practice game too many at home in San Francisco. As a right-hander, he could still pitch, but he couldn't swing a bat and he was unable to move his glove hand more than a few inches away from his chest. As a result our catcher, Ernie McCormick, a retired banker turned serious painter, played under excruciating pressure, for it was his unenviable chore to hit that virtually immobilized glove on the money in each of his return throws to the pitcher or risk hitting Moose with a ball in the face or some even more vulnerable body part. Generally speaking, Ernie held up well under the pressure, but in the sixth inning his return throw completely missed that glove — and, fortunately, Moose himself. I, then in the game at second base, retrieved the ball, but since I was suffering inexplicable throwing problems at the time, my throw back to the pitcher sailed past him once again into Ernie's hands. Ernie, rattled by now, missed Moose once more. I was about to retrieve the ball and start the bizarre sequence all over again when our third baseman, Bob Frugoli, a Square bartender, intercepted the ball and walked to the mound to hand it personally to the now-furious pitcher.

After the Fenway-Wrigley triumphs, Moose was convinced that Les Lapins belonged in big-league ballparks. He was, of course, living out a childhood fantasy: for a few hours every Mother's Day, he was managing a team in the major leagues. And so, at his urging, Brokaw persuaded New York Yankee owner George Steinbrenner to turn Yankee Stadium over to us for the 1987 game. Moose tried to fill us with dread of the opposition once again, but his scare tactics were wearing thin, even with the newer, less-jaded players. Predictably, we trounced Brokaw's bunch 8-1 in the rebuilt House that Ruth built.

Satisfied that he had conquered the best the eastern United States had to offer, Moose turned next to the Orient. Our 1988 game would be played against a team fielded by the Foreign Correspondents' Club there as part of an official San Francisco in Hong Kong celebration. Les Lapins would be part of a delegation headed by former Mayor Dianne Feinstein that would also include the San Francisco Symphony, a motorized cable car, and the City College of San Francisco basketball team. Moose was disappointed that our game would not be held, as tradition dictated, on Mother's Day, but he was proud to be included in such august company. Les Lapins, he admonished us time and again, now represented not just a city but a country; in fact, an entire continent. The pressure was really on this time. And, naturally, our opponents would be the toughest we had yet faced. We should, he advised, take on the aspect of the old St. Louis Cardinals' Gas House Gang, and to illustrate just what that involved, he mailed us a clipping of a contemporary story on the Gang written by Frank Graham for the old *New York Sun*:

"They have thick necks and knotty muscles, and they spit out of the sides of their mouths and rub the backs of their hands across their mouths and wipe the backs of their hands across their shirt fronts. . . . They are not afraid of anybody. . . . They will risk arms, legs and necks — their own and the other fellow's. . . ."

None of us was naive enough to think our manager was kidding. And sure enough, on December 31, 1987, he fired off a warning memo to his players:

> Les Lapins Sauvages: On this day of 1987, our thoughts can go in only one direction — our forthcoming contest in Hong Kong on February 10th. As you know, we are official representatives of the City of San Francisco during San Francisco Week in Hong Kong. . . . Since we will be playing a team already well into its season (they have an ongoing softball league in Hong Kong) it behooves us to *get ready now*. The enclosed practice schedule provides minimum preparation when one considers the possibility of rain-outs. The citizens of our City expect proper representation in Asia. Let's have a good turnout for practice on January 6th. Thanks. Happy New Year. Your Coach.

He enclosed a schedule that called for eight practices in the month of January, a stiff undertaking for men and women with jobs, families, and social obligations. There would be further communications. On January 26, Moose wrote again to "All Members of the Lapins Sauvages:

> As you can see from the enclosed *Hong Kong Standard* story, our team is eagerly awaited there. Practices so far have been fairly well attended and in another month we would be in midseason form but . . . since only a week or so remains before our game, hard work is needed. . . ."

SPLENDID! WHAT'S SOFTBALL?

He enclosed a column written by *The Standard*'s Kevin Sinclair that illustrated, all too clearly, that the writer had fallen hard for our manager's line of hard-luck patter. After extolling The Square as "one of the great drinking spots on the Pacific Rim . . . frequented by lowly forms of life like newspapermen, politicians, policemen, writers, tycoons, real-estate developers, bankers, poets, folksingers, financiers, and wandering adventurers," Sinclair added, "Ed Moose has a few restrictions on team membership. The team must at least verge on middle age, have liver problems, be unfit, include a couple of women (who can be younger and fitter than the men), and not know a hell of a lot about baseball. Above all, players can't take things too seriously. . . . The formation of a team that couldn't care less if they won or lost is a splendid addition to the culture of San Francisco."

Care less, indeed. In fact, Moose had assembled for Hong Kong his best team yet. He had lost power-hitting first baseman Bob Rowell, whose wife wouldn't let him make the trip, and shortstop-outfielder Peter Lombardo, a television producer who is the nephew of the late bandleader Guy Lombardo. And the years had continued to be unkind to the charter Lapins. Sullivan was now confined to a coaching role by an aneurism in his leg that forced his retirement from the police department. Yee had been fired for the after-hours fight he had with Clancy. Dan Bruner, a catcher and first baseman in Paris, had quit the team in something of a huff when it became apparent to him that Caen would get more playing time. Dave Bush, a *Chronicle* baseball writer who had been a relief pitcher in France, had likewise departed angrily after Moose left him out of the Columbia Pictures game. Dorenbush, troubled inevitably by intermittent poor health, had been in semiretirement as team public relations representative since the Southampton game. Jerry McGrath announced sadly that the continuing stock-market crisis would oblige him to stay home for the first time. And the rest of us were just wearing down. Only the absurdly healthy Herb Allen, now in his late forties, was able to play with the old verve. He was also the only one of us who, barring crippling injury, knew he would play every inning of every game no matter what the score. Indeed, Moose would rather forfeit than remove Allen from center field.

Frugoli, a former Red Sox chain third baseman, would make the trip as the third baseman and so would Art Groza, a former Oakland Athletics farmhand. Moose had also added Don Wilborg, a youngish and fit outfielder-infielder who had long starred in Bay Area softball leagues, and Bill Brisbane, a mobile shortstop and sharp leadoff hitter. In short, Les Lapins were loaded, and not at all in the manner suggested by Sinclair's column. Our guys were, for the most part, sober to a fault.

But the Hong Kong media publicized us all week as the bibulous geezers of Moose's advance publicity. Moose himself promoted this image in his frequent appearances on Hong Kong radio and television. Ignoring his stars, he cited Caen, the limping Sullivan, and sixty-five-year-old reserve first baseman Frank Carillo, a heart-disease survivor, as true representatives of Les Lapins. A Catholic priest, the Reverend John P. Heaney, had accompanied the team, Moose said, to deliver last rites should any of our old-timers succumb on the field. In fact, Heaney was a pretty fair ballplayer.

Moose's only pregame mistake was allowing the captain of the Foreign Correspondents' team, Hong Kong journalist Saul Lockhart, to drive him to our practice the day before the game. Lockhart dropped our manager off and stayed at the practice just long enough to see that Les Lapins were not the bumblers Moose had made them out to be. "We've been flimflammed," he muttered. "They've got people who can play." Lockhart did not. One middle-aged Englishman approached one of our players the day of the game and cheerfully announced, "I'm jolly well looking forward to this. It will be my sixth match." The final score was Les Lapins 32, Hong Kong 5. Allen played the entire game in center-field.

Even Moose seemed embarrassed by this lopsided drubbing of the innocents. But not enough, we may be sure, to restore the team to its original lumpish form.

There has been one conceivably beneficial side effect of Les Lapins' rise to softball respectability: the better the team has played on the field, the better it has behaved off it. The newer players obviously take the game more seriously. In fact, they take life a lot more seriously than the rakehells who started the whole thing in Paris almost a decade earlier. The Hong Kong trip was easily the least memorable of all in terms of off-field shenanigans, possibly because most of the players took their wives or women friends along. Our scorekeeper, Patsy Glynn, a widow, was virtually the only unattached woman on our traveling squad. At any rate, not one player took the field there with either a crippling hangover or an oppressive guilt complex. In contrast, not one wife made the Paris trip, and almost every night was a bacchanal. Yee and Dorenbush were missing for several days. And our headquarters, the Hotel Royal Monceau, was the site of a nightly round of musical rooms. In the London half of the 1981 excursion, the DeVere Hotel hired on an extra bartender to attend to us until the last Lapins struggled off to bed, usually around five in the morning. By a rough calculation, the first three softball trips resulted in as many broken marriages. One other marriage was endangered as the result of an affair begun in London, and the Paris trip involved *La Ronde*-type partner switches. Ah, those were the days.

But Moose has had his way. The team looked good. Almost too good. And yet, the peerless leader erred in one specific: that first team was a hell of a lot more like the old Gas House Gang than the last one.

Pretty Pamela Berelson, age 22, is sitting at the bar with her mother, the widow Patsy Glynn. Mike Lipskin is at the piano. "Mom," says Pamela, "you ever get the urge to do something genuinely nutty?"

"Yes," says Patsy, "and I usually do."

"Like what?"

"Oh, like grabbing a microphone like that one and singing."

"You've done that?"

"I'm afraid so."

"Well, that isn't exactly what I want to do. Close, but not exactly."

"Oh God."

"No, I don't want to sing. I just want to go right over to that piano, climb up on top of it, and sit there like Helen Morgan wringing out a dainty handkerchief."

"Don't do it, for God's sake."

"Why not?"

"Because I've done it already."

"You have? When?"

"Like, last night."

"Oh."

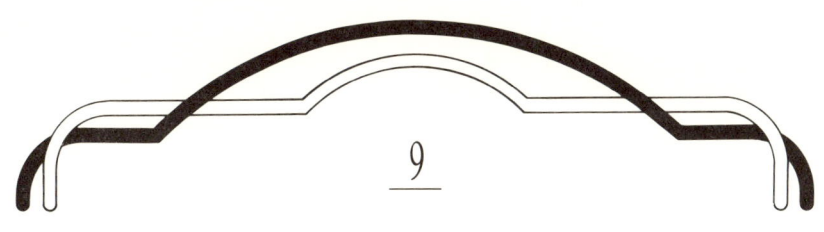

9

Life Goes On and Then It Doesn't

Moose faced a wicked schedule upon his triumphant return from Hong Kong. The Square's twelfth annual Penny Pitch championship was scheduled for Monday, February 22, and softball aside, the big man considers this event the crowning jewel of his social season. The Penny Pitch was conceived by Hal Thunes as a sort of get-together for neighboring saloons. The first one was to be a match strictly between The Square and Zot's, a financial district hangout. But as with so many ideas that begin innocently enough before they find their way to him, Moose picked up the Penny Pitch and ran with it. Competing teams, he decided, should pay an entry fee and the money should go to charity. Moose selected St. Anthony's Dining Room, where Franciscan monks serve down-and-outers in the Tenderloin District, as the beneficiary of his charity. St. Anthony's annual Thanksgiving dinners for the homeless had received national publicity, and they had won enthusiastic support throughout the Bay Area.

The Square held its first annual Penny Pitch championship on Washington's Birthday in 1977. It was a spectacular success. Several thousand dollars was raised for St Anthony's, and the restaurant was packed all afternoon and evening. Thunes was a proud and properly pompous "commissioner," Scott Beach was an eloquent emcee, Sullivan was crowned the first champion, and there was an abundance of the hoped-for newspaper and television coverage.

The event got bigger with each passing year as more and more teams clamored to be a part of it. Most of the Bay Area sports teams (the Giants, the Athletics, the 49ers, the Warriors) entered, as did such rival saloons as Perry's and Mulhern's. Moose arbitrarily set a goal of raising a thousand dollars more for St. Anthony's for each additional year of the competition. Eventually, the Penny Pitch did much better than that. The eleventh annual championship in 1987 raised more than twelve thousand dollars, instead of eleven thousand, and Moose, true to his nature, began setting his sights higher and higher. But because of the Hong Kong adventure, he had been unable to exercise his own personal scrutiny over the 1988 extravaganza. He entrusted this daunting responsibility instead to Sullivan, who upon his retirement from the police department had carved out something of a niche for himself as a barroom social director (he is the chairman also of Mulhern's annual golf tournament), and to Lynn Kennedy, The Square's invaluable office factotum and sister of former mayor Feinstein.

Sullivan is crisply efficient in these matters, a demon fund-raiser whose authoritarian yet hale manner and thunderous voice seem to intimidate even the most parsimonious of potential donors. Lynn Kennedy is one of life's sufferers, a handsome woman who is at her happiest recounting tales of woe. Illness and injury are her stock-in-trade. Maladies of any sort, whether affecting her personally or even complete strangers, reduce her to a grief beyond the comprehension of less sensitive souls. But a large and sometimes bleeding heart does not deter her from a job at hand, and Moose is not above burdening her with a workload that would tax the patience and stamina of a pioneer woman. And yet she accepts these occasionally onerous duties with minimal grousing.

So when Moose returned from the Orient, the biggest of all his Penny Pitches was already in high gear, thanks to the arm-twisting Sullivan and the lachrymose Lynn. And indeed, this one exceeded all expectations, raking in more than sixteen thousand dollars for the good monks and their charity. Mike Sweetow, himself a sometime-restaurateur, triumphed over more than one hundred contestants and became the first two-time champion. The crowd of pitchers, spectators, and disinterested imbibers was the largest ever. Moose was ecstatic, or "orgasmic," as waiter Gary Epting describes him in such moments of rapture. He had won in Hong Kong and, even without his supervision, the Penny Pitch had been bigger than ever.

And yet, big as it is, the Pitch is but one date in a social calendar busier than that of a Midwest Elks Club. Scarcely a holiday or civic event passes uncelebrated by this saloon. St. Patrick's Day is, of course, particularly festive. There is a staff picnic on Labor Day. There is a Christmas and a New Year's party. And on the Thursday before Cal and Stanford play their annual Big Game in November, the Cal Band, one hundred pieces strong, marches into the restaurant, occupies every inch of free space, and blasts out its extensive selection of fight songs and hymns. The band appears courtesy of co-owner Jack Brown, who, though he never attended the university, is such a fan of the school band that he annually contributes thousands of dollars to its support. The Square concert traditionally ends with Brown, round face beaming, conducting the band in encore numbers on Powell Street just outside the front door.

Still, the Penny Pitch is the stellar attraction, and it generally takes days after one of these contests for life to return to normal. The weeks following the 1988 Pitch were deceptively tranquil. Moose and Mary Etta even had time to go to a movie, John Huston's last film, based on one of James Joyce's *Dubliners* stories. They stopped by The Square for a drink after the show. Bartender Al Sharf, surprised to see Mary Etta in the place so late, asked her what sort of momentous occasion had kept her up. "Oh, we've just been to see *The Dead*," she replied. "You have?" asked an incredulous Sharf. "I didn't even know you liked their music."

Art Buchwald, the syndicated humor columnist, dropped by on one of these quiet evenings to play the Match Game with Caen and the *Chronicle*'s own resident humorist, Art Hoppe. In the Match Game the contestants hold three or fewer matches in their hands and try to guess the total number in the game. Despite the wits involved, this particular game was played with great solemnity, for the loser would pick up the dinner tab. A week later, Buchwald wrote Moose:

"Dear Ed: What a fool I am. I didn't realize until after the Match Game was over that there was a mirror behind my chair and both Caen and Hoppe could see what I was holding in my hand. Please don't feel bad about me getting the check. I had to go home to Washington by Greyhound bus, but frankly I enjoyed it."

Tranquil times, yes. Tom Brokaw, who had one daughter at Cal and another at Stanford, stopped in after a visit to both campuses. Novelist William Styron supped late after a lecture. Herb Allen and movie producer Ray Stark flew in for a dinner. And the local chapter of the H.L. Mencken Society held its annual meeting in The Square to toast the memory of the sainted Bard of Baltimore and to hail the fifty-fifth anniversary of Repeal.

Then, after an absence of several years, Stan Getz returned to The Square on Sunday, April 10, to play a benefit for his old friend and former saxmate with the Woody Herman band, Al Cohn, who had died on February 15. It was an unusually hot day, and temperatures inside the crowded, air-conditionerless Square must have surpassed a hundred degrees, but Getz, his bright green shirt black with perspiration, played for more than two hours. He was accompanied by pianist Lou Levy, who is Los Angeles-based but a Square regular nevertheless, and San Franciscans Vince Lateano on drums and Frank Tusa on bass. It was perhaps the finest afternoon of music in The Square's noble history as a bastion of jazz. Singer Pinky Winters, who works regularly with Levy, joined the great tenor saxophonist in sweet and soft renderings of "This Is the End of a Beautiful Friendship" and "It's Over." Money raised from a ten-dollar door charge per person went to the Al Cohn Memorial Jazz Collection at East Stroudsburg University near the Cohn home in the Pocono Mountains of Pennsylvania.

These were sublime moments. They would be succeeded by sad and turbulent times. Even as Getz spun his magic in the warm glow of a Sunday afternoon, an almost palpable sense of foreboding seemed to envelop the place. Moose, who had weeks before strutted like a peacock, now had the look of a man possessed of dark secrets and unsettling knowledge. Indeed, he was already at war with an implacable foe, the restaurant workers union, and he, who loves nothing more than victory, was contemplating defeat. He was also feeling betrayed, for The Square's family feeling that he had so conscientiously nurtured now for the first time seemed threatened. In fact the family had already been torn by tragedy before the Getz concert, and it would soon be torn again.

Tim Lee

Tim Lee had started as a busboy at The Square in 1975. He was yet another of the saloon's Hong Kong immigrants, but unlike so many of the others, he was quickly assimilated into San Fransisco life, an adjustment made easier by his English-speaking cousin, Eva Lee. He also picked up a sense of this new culture from constant reading of newspapers and popular magazines and from watching television by the hour. In a surprisingly short time, he became the ranking celebrity-spotter on The Square staff, the first to detect Joan Rivers in the crowd or Phil Harris or even William Styron. But when in 1978 he was first approached about becoming a waiter, he refused, protesting that his English was not good enough and that, besides, he didn't want to abandon his fellow Chinese busboys by accepting a position above his station. Finally, however, Mark Schachern persuaded him to give it a try.

At first, Tim did stumble over some of the names of French wines, and some of the more exotic drinks did not exactly roll off his tongue. A Tuoca rocks (the Italian liqueur over ice) ordered by Tim sounded more like "two vodka rocks" to the bartenders. And he was sometimes plagued by the more boorish patrons, such as the one who insisted he sing "Happy Birthday" for the amusement of his companions. "Sorry," said Tim levelly, "I do not sing in English." But these mostly inconsequential linguistic hurdles were cleared in time, and Timmy Lee soon became The Square's most beloved waiter, beloved by both customers and colleagues.

He had been, like Yeung before him, a heavy gambler when he first started work, but marriage and children helped him, as they hadn't helped Yeung, steer clear of the Mah Jong parlors. "Marriage calmed him down," says Schachern. "He lived only two blocks from The Square, and when he walked home at night or came to work the next day, he'd peek in to see what kind of business the other restaurants in North Beach were doing. And he'd keep us informed. He was into everything, up on everything. He knew this business inside out. He was the consummate professional. I'd say he was the most stabilizing guy in the restaurant. He was so bright, and one of the most perceptive people I've ever met. He knew who was sleeping with whom. He could spot the marital triangles. And he had the good sense to keep his mouth shut about it. He could razz anybody on the staff and get away with it."

Lee, in fact, was hardly the obsequious Oriental servant. He had a well-honed sense of the ridiculous, and his tongue was sharp and true to the mark. He had hilarious nicknames for most of the customers and staffers. Georgette Kelly, a delightful older woman with blondish hair and a voice that could shatter wine glasses from Table 42 at The Square to the back room at Perry's, was for Lee "Old Yeller." The bald Alan Goldman was "The Dalai Lama." Saxophonist Partee was "Cannonball." Ernie McCormick, who was generally disinclined to go directly home after the Thursday football luncheons, became "Ernie McDormant." The occasionally combative Lynn Kennedy was "Billy Martin." And his boss, quite naturally, was "Moosolini."

Lee was unflaggingly cheerful on the job and unselfishly prepared to fill in for any sick or malingering co-worker. But no one was really close to him. It was said that waiter Bill Oates was the only one to meet Lee's wife, Elena. And in the view of more than one colleague he was a desperately unhappy man, disillusioned with the role he felt obliged to play as jester for the better-off. "It's sad to say, but I think Timmy was a beaten man," says Bobby Ryder. "To him, this was the end of the line. He could see no place to go. And I think he felt his family looked down on him because he was a waiter." Lee was also an asthmatic who on more than one occasion had to take refuge back of the kitchen during an attack.

He had worked his shift on the night of March 15, 1988, and gone home to Elena and his sons, Allen, age eight, and Benjamin, age four. He had had trouble breathing that night, but he had an appointment to see his doctor the next morning so he felt no immediate cause for alarm. But he suffered one final asthmatic seizure sometime during the night, so violent it triggered a fatal heart attack. He was, to the surprise of everyone at The Square, forty-seven years old. He looked ten years younger. Moose sent off a memo to the staff the morning of March 16:

> The death of Tim Lee comes as a shock to all of us who worked with him the last ten years and knew what a special person he was. We will not meet a better friend or colleague. Tim exemplified the spirit of this place in his intellect, humor and professionalism. We already miss him very much.

A wake was held for him at The Square, attended by more than one hundred co-workers, friends, and customers. Ten thousand dollars was raised for the widow and children, five thousand alone from Gary Damveld, a generous brewery executive. His cousin, Eva Lee, spoke for the family and expressed absolute amazement that so private a man could have had so many good friends.

Timmy Lee would probably have enjoyed his wake, but his sense of the ridiculous would have been tickled more by a misadventure at his funeral service. Like all Square staffers, cook Ronnie Barber was a fond admirer of the clever Chinese waiter. Barber is also a sentimental man, so on the day of Lee's funeral in North Beach he felt his emotions could not survive the services without fortification. He stopped by Gino & Carlo's (where he is one of the reigning pool champions) to prepare himself for the ordeal. After an hour or more of remorseful drinking, he set off for the funeral parlor down the street. There, he took his seat and almost immediately began sobbing uncontrollably. His grief was such that he was entirely oblivious of his surroundings. Had he been more alert, he might well have observed that there were no familiar faces among the mourners. But head down and eyes shut tight with tears, Barber filed forward with the others to view the last remains. It was only when he looked down into the open casket that he realized something was terribly amiss, for he saw there not the familiar face of his Chinese friend but that of a bearded old man, quite obviously Caucasian. He had gone to the wrong funeral home and had wept long and hard for a total stranger. Timmy Lee would have enjoyed that little postscript to his life.

Stanton Delaplane

Stanton Delaplane, the *Chronicle* columnist, had over the years become almost as familiar a figure in The Square as Timmy Lee. Timmy and Bill Oates were, in fact, his regular servers, a task that scarcely challenged their waiterly resources since Delaplane was a man of rigidly fixed habits. A couple of stem martinis, the soup and salad of the day, maybe a short Scotch afterward, and that was that. Timmy affectionately called him "Daily Pain." Delaplane would arrive by cab shortly before noon each day and make his way directly to Table 18, across from the piano. His first martini would already have been prepared and placed on the table by maître d' Dick Broderick. The columnist would sometimes be joined by his wife, Laddie, or by his daughters Kris or Andrea, or, more rarely, by his colleague in many journalistic enterprises, Kevin Keating. But mostly he dined alone, stem martini and his morning column set neatly before him.

Delaplane had joined the *Chronicle* in 1936, the same year Caen came to the paper, and he had quickly established himself as a superior craftsman, a clever and speedy rewrite man, and a brilliant reporter in the field, the first in a succession of *Chronicle* "funnymen," writers who could give the dullest or least plausible story a sharp and amusing twist. He won a Pulitzer Prize in 1941 for a series of stories on the "Free State of Jefferson," a proposed forty-ninth state consisting of five counties on the California-Oregon border whose citizens felt put-upon by their existing state governments. It was a serious, if quixotic, movement, and Delaplane covered it with humor and compassion. He won the first of several National Headliner awards in 1946 for his riotously amusing coverage of the amatory exploits of one Francis H. Van Wie, a San Francisco streetcar motorman who, as far as authorities could calculate, had been married eighteen times and never divorced. Delaplane, borrowing from a swing tune of the time, called him "the Ding Dong Daddy of the D-Car Line."

In 1950 Delaplane began writing a column for the *Chronicle*, ostensibly about travel but mostly about anything that came into his head. It was in these pieces that he refined a style distinctive for short, fragmented sentences, archaic jargon, and wily asides. He might in one sentence write about talking dogs and in the very next about growing up on a farm in Illinois and in the next about the ingredients that make up a proper stem martini. If it seemed a stream-of-consciousness outpouring, it was in fact all very carefully crafted. And it worked to hilarious effect. Delaplane had his admirers among writers everywhere, one of them the eloquent British observer of the American scene, Alistair Cooke. The Delaplane style, said Mary Etta Moose, in as apt an analysis as any, "is like a Picasso line drawing. There are internal rhythms to it. You can't touch a line of it without hurting it."

Delaplane was a sparely built, crusty-looking man with a giving nature. He was particularly generous with his time and advice to young newspapermen, many of whom remain forever in his debt. He was quiet, even shy, and though his health had been failing for years, he held fast to his comforting lunchtime ritual at The Square, and he kept writing.

"I cannot," he told Moose one day, "afford not to write." In the column, he portrayed himself as a middle-aged householder perpetually harassed by children, pets, and bill collectors. But he was eighty years old when he died on April 18, 1988, of heart failure complicated by emphysema.

At the wake The Square held for him, Caen read from a tribute to him written by Cooke for the BBC. Abe Mellinkoff, an old Delaplane friend, fellow columnist, and former *Chronicle* city editor, read the obituary Delaplane had written for himself some thirty years before his death:

> The management announces with regret that Mr. Delaplane died yesterday. He walked into his dingy cell and took a look at the typewriter and the inch-thick dust on the dictionary. And he lay right down and died.
>
> For some time he has complained, but as he spent most of his life complaining, nobody paid any attention to it. It is believed that he suffered a severe collapse of fresh material complicated by malnutrition. He was fed crusts of leftover AP and UP filler items, which is a poor diet for a growing boy.
>
> His last words were, "The same, only make it double. . . ."
>
> On his passing he was sure nobody loved him, which unfortunately was too true.
>
> Mr. Delaplane's owners kept him in an airless cubicle that would have looked out on the alley if the windows were not boarded up. The heat was kept on in the summer and turned off in the winter. Each day they kept a man down the corridor beating a hammer on a boiler. His nerves were frayed like an old trouser cuff.
>
> He was cheerful up to the last and seemed to recognize those about him. Recognized them and kept right on walking.
>
> His transgressions were many and his accomplishments few, but he forgave himself freely for both. His friends often remarked that you could say this: He never hit anyone with an axe.
>
> His final moments were distressing. He sat at his desk, for the thousandth time smearing his white shirt with the printer's ink that drifts in with the coal dust from the alley. His mouth fell open and he emitted a smoke-blue statement of two-and-a-half pages double-spaced, most of which cannot be printed in

a family journal.

From some years of being exposed to this drifting ink, he is the color of a ripe bruise, and the casket will be sealed.

Friends will long remember how often they have seen him on his scrawny knees, pleading for warm oats and a better stable. This was regarded by his owners as hilarious and proved he was a humorist. . . .

Yesterday the poor wretch suffered a deflation of spirit matching his finances, and passed to his reward. . . .

His age was uncertain but he was old enough to know better. He is survived by hardier journalists and leaves a stack of unsold manuscripts and an incredible pile of ink-stained white shirts.

The cadaver will lie in state today, probably in the Palace Corner behind a bank of Palm Court salad. Anybody who wishes may view the remains, which will probably be sitting up taking an infusion of Scotch over ice.

Interment will be in Hanno's Corner for gentlemen journalists at Fifth and Mission streets, where the departed spent a good deal of this life and sometimes most of his pitiful salary.

Table 18 at The Square was off limits to all customers for two days after Delaplane's death. But both days there was a place setting on the table, a thin vase of flowers, and one chilled martini in a long-stemmed glass.

"Our Paglia E Fieno is really good today, sir."

"Oh? What's that?"

"Well, it's egg and Spanish noodles with Gargonzola sauce, along with Dolcelatte and Mascarpone cheeses, sweet basil, and toasted pine nuts."

"What else is good?"

"Well, our other special is grilled Gasquet Trout with Pancetta and garlic parsley. It's served with steamed new potatoes. The fresh raspberries are extra. And our soup is ham and barley."

"Uh huh. Anything simpler?"

"Sure. How about some Monterey Calamari Arrabbiata or a Fishermen's Salad of Calamari, Bay Shrimp, and Scallops Vinaigrette."

"Yeah..."

"Maybe you'd prefer our fresh scallops sautéed with Sauce Dill Beurre Blanc."

"Maybe."

"Wanna hamburger?"

"Yeah, that sounds good."

"Coming right up."

10

The Flavor of North Beach

In 1981, Mary Etta Moose and Square regular Brian St. Pierre, a writer and oenophile, wrote a lively little combination guidebook-cookbook entitled *The Flavor of North Beach*. "Flavor" has a dual meaning in these pages, for though the book is ostensibly about food (including recipes and restaurant reviews), it is also about the ethnic and spiritual flavor of this singular neighborhood. North Beach (and it was a beach before land was filled in on the bay east of it) was settled originally in the Gold Rush era by northern Italians seeking not so much the riches that supposedly lay in the Sierra Nevada as a secure base in this burgeoning port city. As St. Pierre wrote in *Flavor*'s introduction, the Italian settlers "worked hard, put down their roots, and sank their money into property, fishing boats, and bringing over more of their own. . . . The hard question of assimilation that faced so many immigrants on the East Coast didn't arise for them, as this was such a new and wide-open society, with so many immigrants all at once, that there wasn't anything much to assimilate into. They tended to Italianize the places they settled, rather than the other way around."

And so, despite an ever-increasing infiltration from neighboring Chinatown, North Beach today retains its distinctly Italian flavor. From the spires of the church of Saints Peter and Paul in the north to the colossal Transamerica Pyramid at the south end of Columbus Avenue, the sons of Italy have left their imprint. And Washington Square Park is their piazza. That it is *Washington* Square at all is just another San Francisco anomaly, because the statue in the center of it is not of the father of our country but of Benjamin Franklin. Sunbathers, secretaries at lunch, Chinese businessmen, bicyclists, even jugglers share space there now with the old Italians, but the dozens of restaurants that fan out from its grassy slopes are predominantly, if not exclusively, of the old country. Young men in black shirts sipping cappuccino sit on the bar stools of the old Bohemian Cigar Store at the southwest corner of Washington Square. The Ristorante Fior d'Italia, established in 1886, and La Felce are at the southeast corner, across the street from each other. Mama's, where the rich aroma of tortellini seeps through the open doors, is a block north on Stockton Street. Across the street from Mama's is the Liguria Bakery. Within just a few blocks are the North Beach Restaurant, Caffe Sport, the Green Valley, the Savoy Tivoli, and the New Pisa. Little City and Amelio's are less than a block from the Washington Square Bar & Grill. It is a neighborhood alive with the sounds, sights, and smells of sunny Italy, and it's been that way for more than a century.

So even though Ed and Sam had considered opening a chophouse, it was inevitable that theirs too should be a restaurant serving Italian food. Aldo Persich, and to some extent his slightly older brother, Marcello Persi, removed any doubt about that. The brothers are originally from Trieste, but Marcello, who had cooked at Pistola's before Ed and Sam took over, had dropped the last two letters of his name to sound more Italian and become better assimilated into North Beach life. Aldo was an excellent chef, but when he wasn't cooking, the customers, as Ed so ruefully acknowledges now, "didn't know what the hell they would get" in the early days of The Square. And Aldo, then in his sixties and in declining health, could not work all the time. As a result, Square food was wildly inconsistent. At least the price was right. A fresh petrale meunière went for only $3.95, a veal scaloppine for $4.50, a plate of ravioli in meat sauce for $3.50 in 1974.

The early reviews from the town's mostly ferocious restaurant critics were not encouraging. Patricia Unterman, a critic who also owns a restaurant, gave The Square a solid knock, despite Ed's angry protests that it was "both unprofessional and immoral" for her to be reviewing a competitor. But even Caen, not yet victim to The Square's ineffable charm, agreed that though the bar of the "Bar & Grill" was fine, the grill was not so hot.

Ed, Sam, and Mary Etta, who was herself a superior cook but with no restaurant on-the-line experience, tried everything and everyone to bring the kitchen up to snuff. They hired Silvio Conciatore, who had been a leading chef at any number of North Beach restaurants. Like Aldo, he proved a positive influence, but he was then in his seventies and he lasted only a short time at The Square. Tullio Rosati restored some discipline to the kitchen with his dictum to the cooks: "The only time you don't come to work is when you're dead." But Rosati had a bad back and he lasted only four years at The Square. John Soo Hoo, a Chinese who cooked Italian and had been the personal chef at different times for General MacArthur and Bing Crosby, was hired. Soo Hoo had had a brutal apprenticeship in North Beach, where Chinese were rarely seen or welcomed in the kitchens of Italian restaurants, and he emerged from it as a tough boss unreceptive to the whims and complaints of younger cooks. And in their ongoing search for the right kitchen combination, the owners had taken to hiring a succession of young hot shots, "California cuisine guys," said Ed, "who cooked too cute." One of these prima donnas made the mistake of crossing Soo Hoo on a busy night and, working the line next to the crusty Oriental, thereafter found himself dodging sizzling particles from the Soo Hoo sauté pan. He quit the next day.

The trouble with the new breed of cook, Mary Etta concluded, was that "they've invested enormous expense in training and must recover it quickly by moving up to sous-chef or chef positions. They are for the most part entrepreneurial, interested in developing their own personal styles, making themselves a commodity marketable at higher prices. This gives us the age of the New Concept. The restaurant in the traditional sense of a comfortable, familiar place filled with like-minded souls, where one goes to restore the spirits, is not part of this new approach. Continuity is not in the vocabulary."

And continuity was what The Square was after. Achieving it was quite another matter. Obviously, hiring a parade of new cuisine kids was not the answer. Training and promoting from within, the owners finally agreed, was, and again it was Aldo who led them down the true road. Manuel Saucedo, a young Mexican from Chihuahua, had been in San

Francisco less than two years when he started work for The Square as a dishwasher almost the day The Square opened. He spoke virtually no English, but he was a hard worker and, as Aldo quickly recognized, a fast learner. With the owners' permission, the old chef took the untrained Mexican under his wing and taught him to cook. Manuel, who had never worked at any job longer than a few months, stayed on at The Square as an enthusiastic apprentice. And, as Aldo's protégé, he cooked in the manner of the master. So instead of hiring high-priced strangers, The Square decided to develop its own cooks. And the kitchen workers, aware now of fresh opportunities, were newly motivated. Like the waiters and waitresses, they pretty much signed up for the duration. Three of the current cooks — Saucedo, who is now the night chef, Edgar Rojas, and Barber — have been at The Square for more than ten years. That, in the volatile world of restaurant cooking, is continuity.

And then, in 1985, Oku was hired as head chef and given maximum authority. "He became the boss of the kitchen," said Ed. "That's the traditional way of doing it. We were doing it the untraditional way, running our own kitchen. Richard is a great teacher. His people are loyal to him."

Gradually, the restaurant critics realized there was more to The Square than drinks, music, and laughter. As early as 1975, R.B. Reed, then the "Underground Gourmet," found some good things to say about The Square's food. By 1982, he was calling the food outstanding and fairly rhapsodizing over the menus, which were now being printed daily. "The pasta, called elicoidali (its shape) was in a ravishing sauce with a fennel-coriander sausage, sweet red peppers, red onions, and Marsala. The spring salmon, barely pink, was choice...." In October 1980, food and wine critic Robert Finigan wrote in his *Private Guide to Restaurants*: "Something remarkable has happened of late at the Washington Square Bar & Grill: the food has improved enormously! No report could make me happier, for I have long admired the WSB&G as one of the few world-class saloons left in the United States.... Most of the menu reminds that we are indeed in North Beach, which means that the accent is Italian.... What about Salad of Roast Duck, Fresh Apricots, Red Onion, Mushrooms Watercress, Romaine with Piquant Pear Vinaigrette? I'm not joking."

And finally, in February 1985, *Gourmet*, "the Magazine of Good

Living," gave The Square a two-page rave. "The dated daily menus blend tradition with new thinking," wrote reviewer Caroline Bates, "offering such San Francisco classics as sautés of bone rex sole and petrale dorata with capers alongside grilled petrale with basil sauce and a gingery steamed petrale. There may be baked yellow and red peppers filled with cheese and fennel sausage one day and a salad of roasted duck leg with muscat grapes and star fruits the next. This is saloon food with real character."

Indeed, by the mid-eighties, The Square seemed to have it all. Its reputation as one of the nation's great saloons was entrenched. And the cuisine, once deplored, was now after years of trial and error being praised in high places. Mary Etta could now boast: "Our recipes are sought after by cookbook authors. They are presently featured in some twenty cookbooks, with two more in the works. They've been featured extensively in the local and national press, including the *New York Times* rotogravure."

Top of the world! So what could possibly go wrong? As it turned out, plenty.

I tell you, it was crowded in there. It was the '84 convention, and the biggies were all there. I think George Will, Sam Donaldson, Peter Jennings, and that whole crowd were at one table. You couldn't get in the door with a shoehorn. Well, we were sitting there by an open window (it was a hot night) and suddenly this guy comes up to me from outside and hands me a glass. "I'm sorry to bother you," he says, "but I can't get through the front door. Would you order me a martini on the rocks and hand it back through here." Now, I'm thinking this is pretty strange, but after all, it was crowded, so I say, sure, I guess so. And then I recognize who this guy is. It's Ed Moose. For Christ's sake, he can't get into his own joint! Now, that's doing business.

11

You're Just Selling Gin

The Square's bartenders have long been fascinated by the amazing catholicity of Ed Moose's taste in cocktails. The boss might start his day with a revivifying glass of bitters and soda (or even, on occasion, straight cranberry juice), then step up to a preluncheon champagne. He will polish off several glasses of cabernet sauvignon with lunch (frequently pasta) and then down a port afterward. If he is in an expansive humor, he might even have a postprandial pink gin or maybe some plain coffee with anisette. Then he'll be off to the Press Club for a swim and a nap. But if he is in a genuinely contemplative mood, he will most often set before himself the house specialty, the "CBA," which is five ounces of coffee, an ounce of brandy, and a dollop of anisette. He was in his CBA mode one late afternoon at Christmastime 1987.

"The restaurant is not making money anymore," he said, staring morosely into the stygian liquid. "We grossed $2.7 million last year and lost $50,000. We do more business per seat than any restaurant in San Francisco. Hell, we do more per seat than the 21 Club in New York. But we still lost money. Instead of a five percent profit, we're down to one percent, and I can remember when it used to be twelve percent. Our labor costs are skyrocketing. We've gone from three union employees to forty-three, and our payroll is $1.25 million. The desired figure for labor costs is thirty-two percent. Ours is forty-one percent.

We were making more money when we charged seventy-five cents a drink. And now we have this union contract thing."

Moose was readying himself for battle. Actually, he had fired his first shot months earlier when, at a victory luncheon for Les Lapins Sauvages after the Yankee Stadium game, he had announced that he was putting The Square up for sale. There were mournful cries of "Oh, no," from Les Lapins and stunned looks from the staffers, most of whom thought this was one helluva way to hear about losing your job. Caen printed a lead item the next day on this altogether shocking development. But the fact was, not many people took Ed all that seriously. For one thing, he set his sale price at a million dollars. A million dollars for a thirty-one table restaurant in a tumbledown building on the fringe of North Beach? C'mon. And as one competing restaurateur remarked after hearing the news, "So, even if you do pay that kind of money, what have you got without Ed Moose? He *is* the Washington Square Bar & Grill. He's what brings in the famous people. Without him you just got an old building. And what if he decides to open his own place down the street? Then you really got a lot of nothing."

But Ed was serious. He was angry at new union demands for wage increases and a significant hike in employers' contributions to the employees' health and welfare plan. He was furious with his own staff for what he considered gross ingratitude, and he was disillusioned by what he perceived as a general collapse of the restaurant business, both in San Francisco and elsewhere. San Francisco, with its proud reputation as one of the world's great eating-out cities, had been particularly affected by the downward spiral. Some of the city's finest and most popular restaurants had quietly closed their doors within the space of just a few years, among them such supposed fixtures as Chez Michel, Cafe Americain, Modesto Lanzone's in North Beach, and the Blue Fox (since reopened at a new location and under different ownership). The old Blue Fox had been a popular spot for more than forty years, and Lanzone's had been a North Beach hangout for close to twenty years. And yet, as the *Chronicle* observed in a May 2, 1988 article, "Why Many Restaurants Are Going Broke in SF," nearly two hundred new restaurants opened in the city between July 1984 and July 1987, bringing the total number in the city to two thousand (some restaurateurs, Moose included, think there are actually twice that many) according to figures released by the State Board of Equalization. Even with clear evidence of decline, impulsive businessmen were still investing in restaurants.

"We are cannibalizing each other," Don Dianda of Doros, a financial district restaurant for thirty-six years, told the *Chronicle*. "Customers who used to come in three or four times a week now come in three or four times a month."

"People seem to be eating out less," said Sam DuVall, owner of Izzy's in the Marina, a chic little restaurant inspired by, but nowhere near like, Izzy Gomez's old joint. "Say a single guy who was eating out five times a week has cut back to four times a week. To that guy, that's not much of a cut. But for a restaurant, that's a twenty percent cut. For a lot of restaurants, you lose twenty percent of your business, you go out of business."

The *Chronicle* survey showed that restaurants were being hurt by the popularity of home video movies, by the health craze, which has people eating and drinking less, and by the proliferation, in San Francisco at least, of low-budget, low-priced ethnic restaurants — Thai, Vietnamese and Korean — that seem particularly attractive to young diners looking for an exotic but cheap dining experience.

Moose, the traditionalist, deplores this depressing trendiness. When he sees a once-steady customer jogging by his front door toting a bag lunch, he has to restrain himself from rushing out to collar the traitor. And when a group of business executives troops in and orders salad and Perrier, he is struck by the urge to send the lot of them packing off to a health-food store. Don't they know you don't come to The Square for your health? You come to have a good time. This is not the San Francisco Ed Moose had grown to know and love.

"The psychology of the city seems to have changed," he lamented over his CBA. "When I first came here, business deals were made over the dice cups. These people used to have four, five, or six drinks and maybe never even get around to eating lunch, but they'd still do business. It was part of the business phenomenon here that after a two- to three-hour session like that, someone would put his pen to a major multimillion-dollar contract. It was a way of life. You weren't considered a real guy unless you could handle five or six drinks. You didn't belong in the executive suite unless you could hold your liquor. We could afford to charge two-ninety-five for lunch when we opened and then make up the difference at the bar. I guess things really started to change about five years ago. Expense accounts were seriously cut back then, and business people began to think twice about entertaining at lunch or dinner. That's when you started seeing all those paper bags. People just weren't taking the three-hour lunches anymore. And there's the health thing. All that Perrier and Calistoga water. And Mothers Against Drunk Driving. Then the insurance costs for restaurants went sky-high and rents went up. And now the labor hassle. All of these things seemed to happen at the same time, and it was just a blow, that's all."

Moose and The Square were spoiled, lulled into smugness, given a false sense of permanence, hit with a euphoria by the amazing business they did in 1984, when first the baseball All-Star game and then the Democratic National Convention brought thousands of hungry and thirsty important people to town. Almost every restaurant in the city profited from this sudden and welcome influx, but none more so than The Square, where business, already on the rise, increased by a phenomenal forty percent. Instead of pulling in seven thousand on a good night, The Square was handling eleven and twelve thousand dollars. Instead of serving one hundred ninety dinners, it was serving more than three hundred. And these newcomers from all over the country, all over the world, were spreading the word back home that there was this fantastic little saloon in San Francisco where famous people and local characters hung out together in perfect harmony, where there was jazz every night, where the bartenders and waiters were sharp and funny, where the owners, a big guy and a little guy, were giant personalities, and where, hell, you could just have a ball. At a time when prices and expenses were markedly lower than they are now, The Square raked in two and a half million that fabulous year. "We concluded," said Moose, "it would go on forever."

But it didn't. It couldn't, really, for not every city hosts a national political convention and a baseball all-star game the same year. But business didn't drop off all that sharply. As Bobby Ryder once said, "If this place has a slow night, you know damn well every other place in town is dead. But they're not making as much money as they used to here, and they're cranky about it. I can't say I blame them."

The blame, in Moose's opinion, belongs squarely with Local 2 of the Hotel and Restaurant Employees Union and the extra hundred thousand dollars or more a year he says it costs The Square to remain a union house. "If we hadn't gone union, we'd be sailing now. We'd be making money and we certainly wouldn't be thinking about selling." The irony of an old liberal like Moose talking like a union buster is not lost on him. When he and Sam Deitsch opened The Square, there was not the slightest doubt in either of their minds that it would be a union house. San Francisco, they knew, had been one of the great union towns, site of one of labor's landmark battles, the dock strike of 1934 that spread throughout the city and culminated in the Bloody Thursday shoot-out on July 5 between police and workers. This was the city of Harry Bridges and his ILWU. It was a city where no politician could succeed without union backing, where union leaders enjoyed celebrity and power. It was a city, unlike Los Angeles, that consistently voted for liberal candidates in national elections.

It would have been unthinkable for Ed and Sam to open anything but a union house. Why, their very first employee, Aldo Persich, had been a staunch union man. A union gave the place form and structure, a framework of working conditions understood by workers and bosses. The employees knew they had protection and reasonable job security, and the employers knew they'd be getting the right people and that wages and hours would be clearly defined. With a union, said Moose, "there are no gray areas." And Local 2, run in those early days by Joe Belardi, was easy enough to deal with. Old Joe was no fiery idealist. He was always ready to negotiate, cut a few corners, make individual exceptions. He and Ed got along famously.

Then, too, The Square's clientele had always been on the liberal side. One of the most loyal customers through the years has been Dave Jenkins of the ILWU, a towering figure in the local labor movement. Hadley Roff, a deputy mayor to both Feinstein and Agnos, is another longtime regular. And the writers and newspapermen who frequent the place, Caen included, are by inclination more liberal than conservative. In the early days at least, it would have been bad for business if Ed and Sam had been too obviously probusiness. They knew also that a turn to the right after they had made some money would make them look like hypocrites. It would also be a radical departure from their basic philosophy. "My old man was a businessman, but he was a big supporter of the union movement in the garment industry," says Sam. "He'd be rolling in his grave right now if he heard me talking the way I have been lately."

What makes them feel less hypocritical is their perception of a change in the union movement itself. Union power, particularly in the restaurant industry, is on the wane, they are convinced. Less than ten percent (Moose thinks it's more like six percent) of the city's restaurants are now union houses. Local 2's real strength is among hotel workers, who make up more than half of its membership. And, says Ed, the nonunion restaurateurs enjoy an enormous financial advantage over the union employers, most of whom want out of Local 2. A nonunion restaurant has, for example, much more latitude in fixing work hours. But the main financial drain on the union houses comes from the union's health plan. Employee benefits that once cost The Square about thirty dollars per person per month now run in excess of two hundred and may soon reach three hundred. "Any insurance company in town can give me a plan with the same benefits for a hundred dollars cheaper," says Ed. "The total operating differential between a union and a nonunion restaurant of comparable size is at least one hundred thousand a year. I tell you, the union restaurant can no longer compete." Not that The Square is cheap. "We're losing at least four grand a month," says Ed, "because our labor costs are fifteen to twenty percent higher than other places. Anybody who works here makes twenty percent more than he could anywhere else. That's one reason we get better people."

One of the principal stumbling blocks in the negotiations with Local 2 had been the union's obligation to its four thousand retired members, who receive the same health benefits as active members. "The union leaders can't take anything away from these people," according to Moose, "because the retired members can vote them out of office. A big part of the extra money we pay into that plan goes to all those retired people. So what we have here are two immovable forces. The restaurants can't afford to be union anymore and the union can't change to meet the changing times because they're stuck with all these obligations. And if the leaders change anything, they're out."

Moose was convinced, however, that the union was vulnerable. Its hold on the restaurant community was obviously weak and slipping; it had, in fact, lost a strike in 1984. It hadn't even been able to organize a street named Union, where from Van Ness Avenue to Fillmore Street dozens of nonunion bars and restaurants, including Perry's, flourish. Many of these places hire young men and women who, says Moose, "will work their asses off until they get in the movies or whatever it is they're after, then leave the business. These people don't even know what a union is."

Ed decided to fight, employing a guerrilla tactic before launching a full-scale attack, or, as he prefers, defense. The Square is incorporated as the Washington Park Corporation. Ed is the president, Sam the vice-president, Mary Etta the treasurer, Mark the secretary, and Jack Brown a director. After the 1986 losses, the officers agreed to take a pay cut, the effect of which was hardly devastating to Ed and Mary Etta and Sam. The independently rich Brown is not a salaried member of the corporation. But Mark supported a wife and three young children on his income from The Square. He was the one true victim of the abrupt decline in the corporation's fortunes.

Mark had always been popular with the staff, from whose ranks he had, albeit swiftly, risen. He, probably more than any of the other owners, considered The Square family. It was a feeling easy to acquire in a workplace where scarcely anyone ever quit or got fired. The Square didn't hire college kids or actors and actresses waiting for a break; nor, conversely, did it take on the sometimes grumpy older men who worked the tables at such tradition-bound restaurants downtown as Jack's and Sam's. Instead, it had a staff, mostly hired by Mark, that was both professional and independent. At The Square everyone had a good time, including those who served. And the longer the staffers stayed on, the stronger was their sense of loyalty to the place.

Ed would test that loyalty at a staff meeting he called shortly after the previous three-year union contract expired, on September 1, 1987. He explained the distressing financial circumstances and told the employees that all of the corporate executives had agreed to pay cuts. The one hardest hit by this cutback, he said, was obviously Mark. To compensate for that loss of income, Ed said, Mark was going to take over a couple of waiter's shifts every week. If he worked the best tables, he could make as much as seventy-five or eighty dollars extra a night.

The reaction to this announcement was scarcely what either Ed or Mark anticipated. As union members, the staff told them, they could not accept such a deal, as presented. The best tables should always go to the waiters or waitresses with the most seniority. Management could not step in and take money from the pockets of employees. Mark would be taking profitable shifts away from union members. What Ed was proposing would effectively scrap the hard-won seniority system.

Besides, several of the staffers suggested, wouldn't Mark find it "demeaning" to step down from the front office and don a tuxedo again to work the floor?

Ed was predictably enraged, and Mark, normally in control at all times, sputtered and fumed. "It was the first time," Mark said, "Ed Moose ever had to tell *me* to calm down." Ed told the staff it was "one hundred percent clear in the contract that an owner can work, and you can't tell me he can't." He was going to hold his ground on this one. He threatened to take the case to arbitration. Finally, after a series of angry meetings, a compromise of sorts was reached: Mark could work his two shifts, as long as they weren't at the premier stations reserved for waiters with the most seniority. Still, the whole affair had left a nasty aftertaste.

"I can't blame Mark for feeling bitter about this," said Arlene Boyle, a union activist. "He must feel like a pawn. He was being used. Besides, he isn't taking those shifts anyway (in the early months of the agreement, he averaged about one shift a week). Our theory is that this was just Ed's way of testing the union."

That it was. And it convinced the combative proprietor that he was involved in a fight to the finish. Obviously, there were bigger issues ahead than the right of an owner to work in his own place, but the employees' hardball stance against their friend convinced Moose this whole business with the union was going to get stickier. "Those people turned on the man who hired them," he said afterward. "My first reaction was to say, 'Hell, I'm gonna sell the fucking place.' I was starting to think this wasn't fun anymore and that maybe I should just get out rather than go through the bloodbath of a strike. This thing split us badly. We had never had this kind of dissension before. It was a time of torment and anguish for all of us. It was threatening to break up our family."

Ed's threat to sell, now more serious than ever, was like a rallying cry for Square fans all over the country. Letters poured in from everywhere. The regulars, those loyalists who spend part of almost every day there, almost tearfully advised Ed that he was not just running a restaurant, he was the custodian of a treasured institution. Moose, angry, discouraged, disenchanted, wasn't so sure about that.

"Well, when you're in the middle of a situation, when you're trying to make something work, you never have time to think of yourself as an institution or anything of the sort. An institution is something that just goes on and on, you know. But hundreds of people have come up to me after I said we were going to sell and told me, just as John Wasserman did years ago, that that's what we have here: an institution. I've had perfect strangers tell me, 'You don't know me, but I love this place. Please don't close it down.' Herb Allen, who is not a sentimental man, has told me to keep going because we've got something special here. Tom Wolfe has urged me to stay open. And so many others. You do feel an obligation to these people who have been loyal to you for all these years. I must say, all of this has had an impact on me.

"But I don't know. After fifteen years, you're less romantic about it. You're tired, basically. Just plain tired. And you think it's not in the nature of the saloon business to be an institution. In this business, you can be well-loved one year and yesterday's joint the next. And you think back and realize that most of the wonderful restaurants, the really famous ones of the thirties and forties, are closed up now, long gone. We're kind of in a period of regrouping around here. We're trying to figure out how to survive. But I have to say that sometimes I just don't see the daylight. And on those days, I think back on what Toots Shor once said: 'You're just selling gin. And people can always buy their gin someplace else.' "

"It's kinda sad, really."

"What is?"

"Well, you know the way we're just sitting here at the bar bullshitting, free-associating. Playing word games. Not talking about anything important, but having a helluva time bullshitting."

"So?"

"I don't know that Moose can do that anymore. Maybe he could once, but not anymore, not since the union trouble. With him now, every conversation has to have a reason. Either that or it has to be with somebody important, like Herb Allen or Tom Wolfe. Maybe he can talk about nothing with those guys, but I doubt it. I think every conversation has to have a reason for him. It has to be headed somewhere. Otherwise, he'll just walk away and say, 'Now, what was that all about?'"

"I see what you mean."

"What I mean is, it seems to me Ed's losing his sense of play, the joy of just plain bullshitting. Lose that and you're in trouble."

"Maybe."

"Now, what was it we were talking about?"

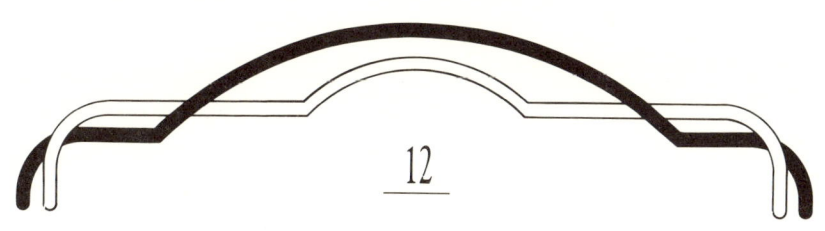

12

Hard Times

Moose was dead right about one thing: The Square family was falling apart. "This is no longer a mom-and-pop store," concluded Gary Epting. "Our boss is not kindly Papa Ed anymore. It's no longer a situation of his taking care of his kids just as long as they're good to papa." In fact, Papa Ed, who had taken to stomping about the premises like some latter-day Gradgrind, looked upon his kids as so many ungrateful brats. And the kids, the waiters and waitresses most active in the union dispute, saw papa as an unfeeling tyrant. These were indeed hard times, and as the battle lines stiffened, The Square began to lose its merry spirit. The man in the middle was Mark. Technically he was a boss, but he had always been a staffer at heart. When people on the floor had problems, it was Mark they turned to, not one of the older men.

"Ed is not a man to give compliments," said Bobby Ryder before he left. "He doesn't make you feel like you've done a good job, but he's very good at telling you when you've fucked up. Thank God for Mark. He's the perfect liaison. He's the one who says thank you."

But Mark, who had hired most of the bright young people now active in the union revolt, was starting to feel, like the well-intentioned Dr. Frankenstein before him, that he had created the instrument of his own destruction. "These are all college-educated people," he said of his staff. "They speak well and they're thinkers. They have the most influence of any who work here. And we take better care of them than anyplace else in town. Still, it's always been our premise that the employees shouldn't tell us how to run our business. My first reaction to what happened after I asked for some waiter shifts was total anger. This has definitely changed my relationship with the staff. I've become more aloof, more skeptical, more negative."

And in ways only slightly more subtle, he found that his relationship with Moose, his boss, mentor, and partner, had also changed, not necessarily to his liking. "When I first came here I was in awe of the man. That relationship then moved to a sort of argumentative partnership. I'd say now that my feelings toward him cover every emotion from pure love to pure irritation. I see him now becoming more and more frustrated. He can't communicate with the staff anymore. Oh, I think we've all decided we've mismanaged this place in some ways and that we've got to tighten up across the board, but this final confrontation has made us all look stupid. It used to be that Ed could go out with us and have a good time, but that's getting to be awfully rare. He and I have fights now over simple things. But there's no question he's the major guy here. He's the one who makes this place go, and he can still work a room better than anyone I've ever seen. And yet, I don't think I've ever met a more complex man. I sometimes wonder if he's fulfilled here anymore. I wonder if he's not more interested in the Herb Allen circle, in politics. I know he'd make a great mayor. He has that anger, that compassion, that love of power and, yes, that Catholic guilt. We just can't afford to lose strong people like Ed Moose. He's what this town used to be all about: color, character, wildness."

Many of the staffers feel Mark became an innocent pawn in Ed's war with the union. And it *was* Ed's war. Of that they were certain, because Sam had been steadily disengaging himself from the day-to-day operations since the bonanza year of 1984. "Sam has no role," says Arlene Boyle. "There's no question any longer that it's Ed's place." Sam pretty much stepped aside by choice. Mark's position seemed to the staff somewhat more ambivalent. "Mark is the guy we all love, but we can't figure out what's going on with him," Arlene said in the heat of the battle. "He would say things like, 'After all I've done for you guys, how can you do what you're doing? You've shut me down.' Well, he's right. He has done a lot for us. But that wasn't the point. The issue was union seniority and playing by the rules. I took Mark out for cocktails once and had a talk with him. I said, 'Mark, we all love you. Nobody's fighting you, personally.' We knew he was unhappy. It's sad, but we started calling him Faust."

For his part, Ed was convinced that Arlene and Marcy, particularly, were being manipulated by Local 2 North Beach field representative Pat Lamborn. "That woman," he said, "had those two in her hip pocket." He was at least half right, for Marcy, raised in the middle class, became a true union activist. She was arrested in union demonstrations outside the hoary Bohemian Club, and she seemed to get as much pleasure from carrying a picket sign as "shucking and jiving" with the customers at The Square. Arlene, daughter of a teamster, was a warier activist. Lamborn, in her opinion, "pushes a little too hard," and the union's sometimes outlandish tactics — parades, sit-ins — rubbed her sense of decorum the wrong way. But both women have felt an increasing sense of isolation since first Sofi and then Judy left The Square and were not replaced by other women. They also objected to Ed's apparent conclusion that the union beef was all Judy's doing. Judy was a vocal advocate of Local 2, they agree, but it was wrong to say it was all her fault, and yet, says Arlene, "You heard that all the time." The two surviving waitresses also felt abandoned by Mary Etta, who in their opinion spent more time worrying about developing trendy dishes in the manner of the renowned Berkeley restaurant Chez Panisse than she did about the fate of Square females. Mary Etta, they said, suffered from "Panisse envy."

It was a criticism that worked better as a gag than as an accurate assessment of the kitchen situation. In fact, Oku had become the boss of bosses there. Mary Etta's influence on the menu, while still an important one, had declined somewhat with the Polynesian's assumption of increased authority. But such remarks were symptomatic of a gathering alienation between the union activists, the vast majority of whom were waiters and waitresses, and management. For employees like Marcy and Arlene, it was an agonizing time. The Square had been virtually a second home to them and a large part of their social life for nearly a decade. For most of that time they had carried on a love-hate relationship with employers who alternately enraged, amused, and charmed them. But that's the way families are, and the two women continued to think of The Square, even through the mounting storm, as family. Why, Marcy had actually gotten her job there because her father had gone to high school with Ed. And Arlene had met her husband there.

And so they went about their daily chores, sustaining a jaunty front, their popularity among customers undiminished by the in-house turmoil. But they were both torn by conflicting loyalties. Marcy, the freshly incarnated labor firebrand, was convinced that the only real issue in all of this trouble was the preservation of the union. The health plan was essential to Local 2's survival in the restaurant industry. If Ed were to have his own way, the union's already fading power in that business would be damaged, possibly beyond repair. And if the employees should agree to an alternate health plan instituted by the owners, they would in effect be, as Marcy called it, "putting all of our eggs in one basket: Ed's." At the same time, she was frightened by the prospect of a union victory dealing a deathblow to The Square. It was as if she were a major player in some sort of Shakespearean tragedy.

"God, I don't want the house to go down," she said quietly after lunch one day. "There's not a person working here who wouldn't go along with some cost-cutting policy to keep the doors open. This is the best restaurant job in the city. Look at me. I'd never had a job anywhere else that lasted more than a year, and here I still am. I didn't grow up in a blue-collar background, and I think unions may well have outlived their usefulness in a lot of industries, maybe ours included, but this issue has to be dealt with."

And hovering over the entire dispute was the towering and enigmatic figure of Ed Moose. He had become, Marcy felt, her enemy, and she his. But there was a bond there, nevertheless. "He can be so incredibly charming, I just can't believe it. I've never seen anybody quite like him. And I'm indebted to him. He's made it possible for me to have the lifelong friends and the lifetime memories I now have. . . . Still, I just happen to think he's a poor businessman. . . ." She laughed softly as a completely unrelated thought passed through her mind. "You know, it's funny, but the guy really has beautiful hands."

Arlene was similarly agitated. Surely, she thought, there must be other ways of paring expenses. No one wants The Square to go under, not even the union, which could scarcely afford to lose another restaurant from its fading ranks. Arlene was sitting on the porch of her Victorian house in San Francisco's Western Addition district one day recently, attending to her two-year-old daughter, Emily, and looking less like a labor activist than a pretty young mother. "We're sympathetic that Ed may be losing money and that he might even resent us because we on the floor are making money while he's losing it. But he sees us as fighters, so he's battling us. He communicates with us now only through nasty memos. He'll take the bartenders and the maîtres d' to lunch, but never the waiters. Still, we're professional people, and none of this affects our performance on the floor."

She lifted Emily to her lap, her silver hair tumbling over the child's small shoulders. "I'm really sad. This has always been such a really sweet thing. I just don't want to think about being without the guys I've worked with for all these years. There's a lot of tension now. I sometimes feel Ed hates me. And yet the other day, I was filling in working as a bartender, and he came by and said, 'How nice you look behind our bar.' I was really touched. But he can't stand to be challenged. To him, everything's our fault. But we're not the reason the place is for sale. If he's not making money, then shame on him. He gets more volume of business than any place in town. And certainly more press. Sure we cost him more than he likes to pay, but we're not the ones putting him out of business."

A late-afternoon breeze had turned the porch chilly. Arlene got up to go inside. "I've always been more than curious about Ed. He can be so charming sometimes. He used to listen to us, ask for our advice, and seem to value what we had to say. But he can be such a child, stomping around when his team loses. There are times when he acts almost as if Mary Etta doesn't exist, then I'll hear him talking on the phone to her and he's really sweet. He's calling her honey and sweety and babe. The thing is, he doesn't want anybody to know this side of him. But strange as Ed is, nobody on his staff wants to screw him out of his place. We know we've got something special here. You hear it all the time, but it's true: for us, this is family."

It was a recurring refrain during those bitter months: This is family; we love this place; we don't want to shut it down. "Ed has done so many good things, like that fund-raiser for Timmy Lee's family, that it would be a tragedy to have this come to the ultimate showdown," said Jim Gallup, whose union activism had set him at odds with his boss. But the threat to sell or close the place was real. "I get the feeling the heyday is over," said Bobby Ryder, making his own plans to leave. Moose all but confirmed this melancholy assessment. There were five ways out of his fix, he concluded: (1) The union could allow The Square to introduce its own health plan; (2) the staff could vote to drop out of the union; (3) Ed and the other owners could simply close the restaurant, gaining no profit from a sale but suffering no more losses; (4) they could declare bankruptcy; and (5) they could sell, in which event the place would inevitably go nonunion, the current staff would be dismissed, and The Square as it had been would be just another chapter in San Francisco saloon history.

Selling seemed to be the most feasible of all these possible solutions, and every week the rumor mill coughed up a new buyer. One prospective owner, Norman Hobday, kept the mill going almost single-handedly. But Hobday is an inveterate self-advertiser and one of the most curious figures in the local bar community. When he ran a fern bar singles hangout called Henry Africa's, Hobday himself assumed the role of the mythical Henry, costuming himself in broad-brimmed hat and safari jacket and affecting the manner of a Great White Hunter. It would have been just good theater if Hobday had played his part only in the bar itself, but he apparently enjoyed the deception so thoroughly that he was Henry Africa all the time. For a while there, Norman Hobday ceased to exist, except on paper. To his credit, Hobday eventually abandoned his disguise, and when he opened a new place, The Dartmouth Social Club, he had the good taste not to appear in public looking like a refugee from a Fitzgerald novel. And as yet, he has not been seen in grease-stained goggles and flying helmet on the premises of his newest establishment, Eddie Rickenbacker's, in the suddenly fashionable South of Market part of San Francisco.

When the hot Hobday rumor reached Mulhern's, where many Square patrons retreated during the labor strife, a chill traveled the length of the bar. What might such a character do to the lovely old Washington Square Bar & Grill? "I'll say one thing," said a distraught Sullivan, "if he's in, I'm outta there for good." But Hobday was not in. Moose was still in command. But what had been the happiest bar in town was now suffused with gloom and uncertainty.

"I find all this very depressing," said Mark Schachern, nervously fingering his own CBA after lunch one day. "I'd feel terrible if we ever had to close this place. I've had trouble sleeping nights. I feel like I'm on a downhill graph. We were on such a roll for five years we thought it would never end. I know all of this is driving my wife crazy. She wants me out of there before it really makes me ill. But it's hard for me to leave because I still believe this is the best joint in the best town in the world. There's nothing around like it anymore. The town needs it. It would be a tragic blow for us to lose this place. You know, I just can't imagine not being here anymore. From the day I first started I thought I'd be here the rest of my life."

Moose is even more agitated than usual. He paces nervously before dropping into his usual seat at Table 42.

"You know what they've done now? I tell you, this time they've gone too far."

"Who's done what?"

"The waiters. Everybody's friends, the waiters. The people you talk to all the time. This time they've gone too far."

"So what did they do?"

"I'll tell you what they did. They stole Mark's tuxedo just before he was to work a shift. Then they left a nasty note behind. 'Fuck you,' it said."

"You're kidding?"

"Kidding! No, that's where things have gotten to around here. Now they're stealing. That's a criminal offense. We know who did it. We're hiring a private eye. I never thought it would go this far, but it has. I mean, this is what we're up against. This is criminal behavior."

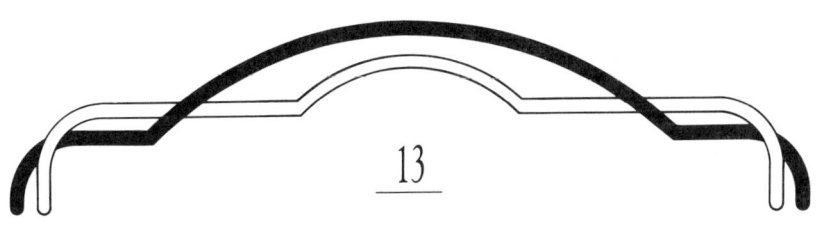

13

We Shall Not Be Moved

In challenging Local 2 of the Hotel and Restaurant Employees Union, Ed Moose had taken on a large, potentially powerful, and certainly unpredictable opponent. The largest union in the city, Local 2 represents nearly thirteen thousand workers, eight thousand in hotels, four thousand in somewhere between two hundred and three hundred restaurants, and seven hundred in private clubs, including the august Bohemian. It also provides benefits for those four thousand retired members. Its restaurants include, in addition to The Square, such culinary shrines as Jack's, John's Grill (where Dashiell Hammett once hung out), the Tadich Grill, Fior d'Italia, the Buena Vista, Trader Vic's, and Scoma's on Fisherman's Wharf, most of which, like The Square, have had a consistently disputatious relationship with it. One would think a juggernaut like Local 2 would be invincible in any labor confrontation, but such has not been the case. In 1984, for example, the union, led by the ideologue Charles Lamb, struck thirty-seven restaurants and came away a loser, retreating from its positions in disarray. The strike was ill-conceived and disorganized, and the union leaders who lost it were summarily deposed.

But that was then, and restaurateurs falsely emboldened by the 1984 victory learned to their grief that under new president Sherri Chiesa, a former bartender, Local 2 is a much more unified and stubborn opponent. In fact, as now constituted, Local 2 seems to be a peculiar amalgam of a civil-rights organization, a revivalist church, a college fraternity, and the Wobblies. "The leadership," says Bobby Ryder, "is very gung-ho." There are songs and cheers at the meetings, and the tactics employed against the union's capitalist adversaries combine civil rights zeal and conviction with undergraduate hokum. In its campaign to bring the Bohemian Club to heel, which it did, the union had members prowling the exclusive Pacific Heights neighborhood, where many Bohemian Club members live, in safari costume, complete with binoculars and pith helmets. It was all very symbolic, of course, a hunt to bring down the lion of privilege, but it looked to Pacific Heights neighbors to be nothing more than some ill-conceived costume party, just another gathering of San Francisco crazies. The union caused a somewhat greater stir, however, when members blocked the hallowed entranceway one day to the old club on Taylor Street. Thirty-three of them, including Marcy Campagne, were arrested.

In another demonstration, some five hundred members of Local 2 held a "multidenominational prayer service, conducted by twenty ministers and priests," at Fisherman's Wharf, where a number of restaurants were holding out against new contract demands. Chiesa, standing like Lord Nelson at the helm of *Victory*, addressed her troops from the deck of a fishing boat docked at the wharf. She also read a letter of support from Mayor Agnos, whom the union endorsed in the 1987 election and who, for several reasons, could be counted on to back it in any campaign against The Square. Ed Moose's joint, after all, represented power and privilege to this champion of the underdog.

A Local 2 tactic restaurateurs find most unpalatable is the so-called dinner-a-thon, in which union members descend on an opposing restaurant, occupy every available table, and remain seated for hours toying with nothing more expensive than a bowl of soup. Moose said that if the union ever pulled one of these stunts in his joint, he wouldn't be responsible for the consequences.

Actually, the membership seems somewhat divided over the efficacy of such bizarre tactics. Jon Palewicz, a hotel worker and longtime union member, told the *Chronicle* he thought Chiesa was turning union protest into "a television show." There is some division among The Square's union members, too. Arlene considers the dinner-a-thon more inflammatory than effective. But Marcy thinks such pranks are, for the most part, "neat." Some traditional labor movement people are aghast.

Others consider Local 2's approach reminiscent in its own curious way of glorious campaigns waged in the thirties by the International Longshoremen's and Warehousemen's Union, in the forties by the United Auto Workers, and in the sixties by the United Farm Workers. As a matter of fact, trendy Local 2 does include among its musical selections some old labor songs as well as civil rights hymns. "We are here for justice, we shall not be moved," members sang at the Wharf. They also chanted, "One, two, three, four, we're outside the door. Five, six, seven, eight, now it's time to negotiate." Union pamphlets and fliers are aflame with such old-time inspirational messages as "be part of the power" and "follow the path to victory." General Patton might have liked Local 2, the "path to victory" part of it, anyway.

Some labor people see Local 2 as the wave of the future, the one great hope for reviving the movement in a city that was once a major seat of union power in this country but has since backslid. "Local 2 is the model for all of us," Steve Neuberger, political director of Local 790 of the Service Employees International Union, told the *Chronicle*. "It may be the ILWU of the mid-eighties." The union's potential for power is certainly there, particularly since it is estimated that by the end of the decade there will be another forty-five hundred hotel and restaurant jobs to be filled in San Francisco, filled, labor leaders hope, by Local 2 members. The union is also well represented by minority and women workers. Forty-five percent of Local 2 members are women. Thirty percent of all members are Asian and twenty-eight percent are Hispanic, no small consideration in a city of such ethnic diversity.

The union asked for a twenty-five-cents-per-hour raise for all employees in the new contract, but the most controversial issue in negotiations with The Square and some fifty other restaurants and clubs whose contracts had expired was an increase in contributions to the Health and Welfare Fund. The union wanted employers to raise these contributions by twenty-five to thirty dollars a month per employee, or to approximately two hundred twelve dollars a month per employee, a figure Moose, for one, considered outrageous. "I support my entire family on a health plan for half that," Mark Schachern says.

The union, on the other hand, considered this proposed increase modest, a "hold-the-line" figure in the face of hospital costs that, according to insurance company figures, have increased seventy percent in five years. The high incidence of AIDS has also significantly raised the cost of health insurance in San Francisco. "Health care is a national scandal," says field representative Pat Lamborn. "I know that every employer in town says he can buy a cheaper plan, but I also know a lot of them have had to eat their words. You just can't get a better package for the price."

Local 2 sees its health plan as having several specific advantages over other, possibly cheaper, plans. For one, the employee has a choice of three different medical and dental plans. And if the employer should be delinquent in his contribution (ninety-one percent of all San Francisco restaurant bosses have been delinquent at least once in the past, the union says), the Health and Welfare Fund will pay for the health care anyway, dunning the employer for the missing contribution. All medical, dental, pension, vacation, and sick leave benefits continue uninterrupted if the employee should change jobs and move to another union house. He loses them all, of course, if he drops out of the union. And the Fund provides health care for life for all eligible pensioners and their dependents. The plan also has a built-in enforcement factor that allows the union to audit the employer's books and check on delinquencies. These "administrative costs" also figure into the increase the employers are being asked to pay. But the total increase, the union says, will add up to only fourteen cents per hour per employee.

Moose and many of his fellow restaurateurs strongly objected to the money paid out from the plan to the four thousand retirees. An owner can hardly balk at providing health protection for his own employees, but why pay, owners say, for thousands of persons who have nothing to do with them? "San Francisco is famous for being a great restaurant town," says Lamborn. "And that reputation, which helps the people now running restaurants, was made by those people who have retired." So, she says, they're entitled to all they can get.

It is Lamborn's predictable view that it is the workers who make or break a restaurant, not the bosses. She does have a point, particularly in regard to The Square. Here, every day, there are familiar faces, recognizable personalities standing by to serve the patrons. And they all have their fans among the hundreds who pass through those doors daily. Moose himself tells of a customer who stopped in for lunch several days after Timmy Lee's death. "Where's my favorite waiter, the Chinese fellow?" the customer asked. When told that Lee had died unexpectedly, the man seemed shattered. "Did he have a family?" he inquired.

Moose said he did, a wife and two young sons. "Here then," said the customer, handing Moose a hundred-dollar bill. "Maybe this will help them."

In San Francisco, at least, imbibers have been known to follow their favorite bartenders from job to job. Losing a bartender would be like being deprived of a close friend and confidant. Still, Lamborn, who could hardly be considered an objective observer, was off the mark when she overlooked the inestimable importance of an inspired and creative boss like Ed Moose. Moose is the dominant personality in his saloon. He, more than any of his employees, gets people in the place. He *is*, as his competitors ruefully admit, the Washington Square Bar & Grill.

But to Lamborn, he was just another boss, and that is a generic term in her vocabulary. All bosses are the same. And none can be trusted. "We've looked at the books in some of these places," she says, "and we've seen all the accounting errors. We've corrected their bookkeeping for them. We actually provide a service by standardizing wages and benefits. Without us, there'd be none. People who run restaurants are not all good businessmen, and they do direct their profits elsewhere, outside the restaurant. OK, so if they tell us the increases we're asking for are the difference between their staying open and closing, let us look at the books, then we'll negotiate."

Lamborn is a small, dark woman in her middle thirties. She started working on the assembly line of a nonunion electronics plant in Santa Clara County, south of San Francisco, in her early twenties. Long hours, low pay, short vacations, and frequent personnel turnovers there convinced her of the need for unions. She became a labor organizer in 1978 at age twenty-three and has been at it ever since. She joined Local 2 in April 1987 and was assigned to North Beach as an organizer and field representative. Her only previous experience in the restaurant business had been as a cafeteria worker. She does not regard this as a handicap, however. "It is much more critical to have experience in the labor movement than in the business itself, and I've got that."

She goes about her work with the enthusiasm of a high-school cheerleader, which is exactly how many of her foes see her. Mark Schachern speaks of her bitterly as "my friend." Ed merely rolls his eyes and mutters silent curses at the mention of her name. It is a dark moment for him when he spots her bustling through The Square's front door, her arms filled with inflammatory leaflets. "I'm afraid Pat and Ed are oil and water," says Rick Snyder. For a time, Marcy and Arlene treated her as a chum, inviting her to social occasions, including Scott Beach's annual birthday party at Monroe's, a union restaurant that, because of owner Peter Lomax's close friendship with Moose, was alien territory for her. But Lamborn is apparently unaffected by any hostility directed her way. She seems almost girlish, even giggly girlish, on first meeting, but there is a steely resolve beneath this deceptive façade.

Lamborn and the other officers of Local 2 do say they are aware of The Square's unique status in the restaurant community. And they do see it as something of a special case. "Part of this whole situation is how the workers see themselves," says Peter Cervantes-Gautschi, a former United Farm Workers organizer who is Local 2's staff director. "If a waiter sees himself as a rock singer or an actor just doing this for a couple of years until he makes it, he doesn't have much of an investment in the industry. But the Washington Square is a different matter. People stay there. They are interested in quality performance. It's their profession, and they want to maintain the quality where they work. That's where we come in. I'd be surprised if the employees at the Washington Square believed that a nationally famous restaurant like theirs was going broke. All you have to do is go there on a Friday night. Now, our health plan is central to our union, because one of the most important things in a union contract is security and building seniority. There's a big difference between what a waiter can make at a Tuesday lunch and a Friday dinner, you know. We want to help our people build a future that won't change as the wind blows or at the mood of an employer. We think it's better to have one deal, one citywide health and welfare package."

It is technically possible, Cervantes-Gautschi concedes, for a restaurant to separate itself from the health and welfare package and still remain union in terms of wages and working conditions. "That could happen, yes, but I don't think it will. The city has backed us on this. They don't want to see new clients on welfare. Look, we know we're being tested. We had a disastrous strike in '84 that was bad for the entire industry. Workers lost their jobs and some places went out of business. That was a lose-lose situation, a horrible strike. But now the facts of life are somewhat different. An owner now is not just fighting his thirty or forty employees, he's fighting twelve or thirteen thousand people. And it's the workers who decide whether they are union or not. It's not the owners."

And if Moose, as he threatened to, should sell to someone who would fire all of the current employees and hire only nonunion workers, effectively eliminating the union from the picture, what then? "We'd picket," said Lamborn. And what if The Square should just disappear? What if a grocery store should take its place? The union would then be minus one of its showplaces, wouldn't it? "It wouldn't make a lot of sense to take that rickety old house and make it into anything else, would it?" said Lamborn. "As I see it, the Washington Square Bar & Grill is a business, sure, but it's also a landmark. It has a politically liberal tradition. Union people go there, journalists, Democratic politicians. Being a union house only enhances its image. The union gives it stability. It insures that its creative employees will stay there. I'd be surprised if The Square wanted to have a war. We expect a good outcome."

Reggie Jackson is having a beer at the bar with his lawyer, Steve Kay, when they are approached by a casually dressed young man in his early twenties. Reggie looks at Kay and rolls his eyes. Here we go again. Guy probably wants an autograph for his younger brother. Maybe wants to buy a round of drinks. Gotta unload him fast. But the young man stops just short of the two, gives a little wave and says, "Hi Reg, just wanted to say hello." Reggie looks puzzled. He turns to the lawyer. "Do I know that kid?" "Reg," says Kay, "that was Will Clark. Plays first base for the Giants." "Oh, right."

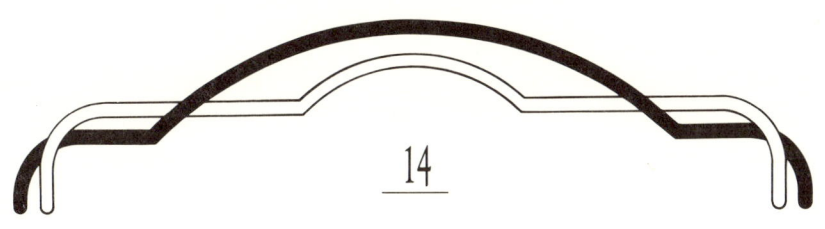

14

The Future Is Now

To know Ed Moose is to expect surprises. The man has an abiding distaste for the predictable, a positive dread of fulfilling expectations. He subscribes enthusiastically to Emerson's tart observation that "a foolish consistency is the hobgoblin of little minds." This characteristic is well known to his employees, the keenest of whom start their day by trying to read their boss's craggy face for clues of what joys or horrors lay ahead. And yet when in mid-July 1988 Moose agreed to sign the new union contract, jaws fell in the negotiating room. "My first reaction was to look around for a pen," said Arlene Boyle. "I couldn't believe it." But Moose, whose distaste for Pat Lamborn and members of the employees negotiating committee (principally Marcy, Arlene, Rick Snyder, and Jim Gallup) had grown to a teeth-gnashing rage, had managed to hammer out a compromise agreement, working in concert with Local 2 head Chiesa. Lord knows, he wasn't happy with it, but it was, he concluded, something he could live with for however long it took him and his partners to sell the place.

According to the agreement, The Square would accept the health-plan increases — twenty-five dollars per month per person increases for three years — bringing the restaurant's contributions for each employee to two hundred eighty-eight dollars a month by 1991. In return, wage increases of twenty-five cents per hour would go only to union-scale, nontipped employees, mostly kitchen help; paychecks would be received every two weeks instead of weekly; uniform allowances for waiters would be dropped, a savings of more than four thousand dollars per year; all employees would give up one holiday, Washington's Birthday, the day of the Penny Pitch; and Mark Schachern would be permitted to work his two waiter's shifts at top seniority stations. The savings agreed to, said Ed, would amount to perhaps ten thousand dollars a year and would "put off the moment of truth, the ultimate disintegration of the whole history of this restaurant."

The alternative to signing, he said, was an informational strike, in which union members who did not necessarily work at The Square would descend on the place and start up their infernal chanting and singing outside, harassing customers as they had in previous demonstrations in front of the Bohemian Club and the venerable Jack's restaurant downtown. "Our employees would get paid, and the restaurant would slowly bleed to death. It would have destroyed this restaurant, because we would not have stayed open to see it."

Not that the compromise ensures the future of the place. "No, the economics of it just won't work," said Ed. "I told the union that signing this contract will ultimately result in the closing of this restaurant, that it will be a disaster for everybody who works here. And do you know what the negotiating committee said to that? They said, 'Be that as it may. . . .' Be that as it may! Can you believe that?"

The Square, he said, is still for sale, even though no "acceptable" offer has yet been made. The impact of the health-plan increases won't be felt until sometime in 1989, he said, but in order to meet the cost, "we're looking at charging four dollars for a drink or eight dollars for a hamburger. The union restaurants just can't compete with the nonunion places. When we started in this business, eighty or ninety percent of the joints in town were union. That's down to six percent now, and within three years it will be down to zero. Every restaurant like ours will be sold or go bankrupt. Everybody knows what will happen, but nobody can do a thing about it. It's like a Greek tragedy, I tell you."

The Square's four corporate officers will take another ten percent salary cut, Ed said. "And Sam will retire pretty soon, no matter what. For him, the thrill is gone. Some of the prospective buyers have said they want Mark and me to stay on as employees, but I don't know about that. In fact, I don't know what I'll do when the time comes. Maybe I'll go back to school or possibly do something for Senator (Bill) Bradley. I know one thing — you need to get a lot of fun out of the restaurant business to put up with all the rest, and I've found myself getting crabby. I know I don't look at the staff in the same way, and I'm sure they don't feel the same about me."

Strong words. And a bleak forecast. But Moose's behavior after he agreed to sign the contract (which actually took place on August 11, two days after the union signed) was hardly that of a man staring into the abyss. In fact, some of his old demonic energy seemed to have been restored. And the imagination started working again. He began booking jazz acts for Sundays, planning birthday parties, planting column items. For the first time all year, he published the *Washington Square Bar & Grill Gnus*, the gossipy little newsletter he mails to customers all over the country. Caen ran three-column items on the *Gnus* the very week it appeared in July, defending his right to call The Square "the Washbag." And the Sunday *Examiner-Chronicle* magazine section ran an item on the fact that this particular edition of the *Gnus* ran four obituaries — for Tim Lee, Delaplane, former magazine editor Hal Silverman, and Georgette Kelley's husband, Bob. For a man making angry noises about packing it in, Ed Moose was sounding much more like a man back in business.

If further evidence of that were needed, the *Gnus* announced plans for a Lapins Sauvages rematch in North Beach with the Hong Kong Foreign Correspondents Club and a tenth anniversary game in the Bois de Boulogne against Le Moulin du Village. In fact, Moose was planning his biggest softball extravaganza of all for Mother's Day week in 1989. Not only would Les Lapins play again in Paris; they would also travel to Moscow for a game against an all-star Soviet team to be assembled by journalist and baseball enthusiast Vladimir Pozner. Pozner, who lived for many years in New York and speaks virtually unaccented colloquial English, had dinner with Moose and Caen to complete arrangements for this international classic, a game Moose now portentously referred to as the ultimate expression of peace and goodwill between the United States and the Soviet Union. Pozner, who attended a Lapins practice later that week, was equally enthusiastic about the peacemaking possibilities of such a match. Caen diplomatically did not advise him that several innings of Ed Moose on a softball field in Moscow might well lead to a full-scale resumption of Cold War hostilities.

But even without the Moscow plans, The Square's boniface was looking and acting like his old self again, and even he, in perhaps a weak moment, had to confess, "Maybe after all, I'm being just a little too pessimistic about the future of this place." Maybe.

"Excuse me, Miss, can I get you a drink?"

"Oh, I don't know. I just dropped in to meet a friend."

"Sure, but a little drink wouldn't hurt."

"I suppose not."

"Neil, would you get the lady whatever she's having. And I'll have my usual. On the rocks."

"You must come here often."

"My favorite place in this town. Actually, I'm from Boston."

"You are? Hey what a coincidence. That's where I'm from."

"No kidding. When did you move here?"

"Just last month."

"From Boston. Well, I'll be damned. Next time you get back there, say hello for me to old Weasel MacDougald. What a guy."

"Who?"

"Weasel MacDougald. What a guy."

"I'm sorry. I just don't know . . ."

"Hey, are you sure you're from Boston?"

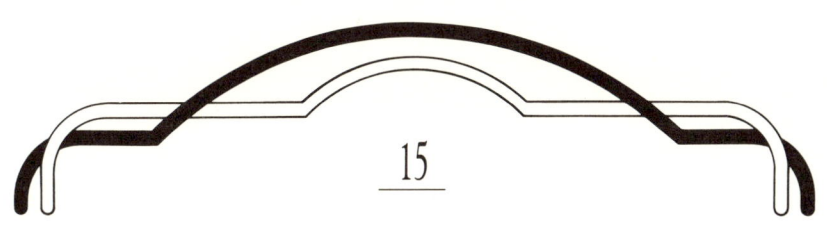

15

Good Night, Sweetheart

At night The Square is quite a different place. The light seems softer, the sound more muted, the faces less distinct. The jazz piano makes it less of a talker's place than a listener's. The crowd is not so well dressed. And the drinking is heavier. The sense of community is not as strong at night as at noon, when the regulars assemble. At lunchtime, The Square is a club; at night it is a refuge. And when the sun sets, the local color comes out. There is Millie, the tiny toothless flower woman who patters from table to table peddling her wilted wares, plucked, it is said, from graveyards. Millie will also take your photo out of focus, for a price, with her battered Polaroid. She is a character from the Great Depression, a seedier Apple Mary. And if she is not exactly loved by staff and patrons, she is at least accepted as a slightly disreputable member of the extended Square family. Then there is the man called The Grinder. Perhaps five feet tall, he is not much taller than Millie and is much slimmer, and he too works the room. But The Grinder has nothing to sell but himself. He just likes to talk, to grind out conversation, with anyone patient enough to listen. Unlike Millie, he is immaculately dressed right up to the snap-brim hat he never removes, and his manner, if not his conversation, is that of a *boulevardier*. It is not always easy to catch the drift of The Grinder's message, for by the time he is ready to make his rounds, he has generally fortified himself to the point where his speech is less than distinct. He did make himself clearly understood one night, however, when bartender Frugoli attempted to shoo him away from a couple obviously unreceptive to his discourse. The Grinder looked up at Frugoli, who stands about six feet three and weighs maybe two hundred twenty, and fixed him with a look of contempt. "Young man," he said, "don't let my size intimidate you."

Nighttime at The Square is Neil Riofski time. A bartender at The Square since 1978, he was tutored in the hard school of those old princes of darkness Tom Slater and Hal Thunes. "That was a tough crowd," says Neil. "They'd hit the green Chartreuse about ten o'clock and go on from there. I was just the kid from the Richmond District, a real lightweight." Neil survived Slater's sometimes cruel hazing, and the two eventually became bosom pals. When Slater sold a restaurant he once owned on Long Island and moved for a time to Sarosota, Florida, Riofski regularly joined him and his wife there on vacations. And when Slater finally returned to San Francisco and, at least part-time, to The Square, he and Neil, in the time-honored way of all bartenders, began formulating plans to open their own joint someday. Their only problem, they concluded, would be finding somebody to keep an eye on the place during the day, since neither of them could function when the sun was out.

It is 'round midnight at The Square. The dinner crowd is long gone. Millie has made her rounds, and so has The Grinder. Frugoli is serving CBAs to a youngish couple in brow-to-brow conversation at the far end of the bar. Neil is ringing up the checks for the night and sharing philosophical asides with Tommy, the cabdriver and horseplayer, and Specs Simmons, who is taking a break from his own saloon, Specs', up the street. Neil, like so many of The Square's people, is of a literary bent. He graduated with a degree in English literature from the University of San Francisco, class of '69, and did graduate work at UCLA. Although he faithfully kept a journal and dabbled, as pal Slater had before him, in writing short stories, his career as an author never really took hold. But his welcoming speeches at his own Christmas birthday parties (he was born December 23, 1948) are uniformly brilliant, and he is The Square's poet laureate at parties and special occasions, an honor he once shared with Judy Berkley.

Neil was born in New York, but his family moved to California when he was just seven years old, and he is basically a product of his San Francisco neighborhood, the Richmond District. His hoarse speech has a New York edge to it, which is not at all uncommon in certain San Francisco neighborhoods. But the street-smart talk is the only thing tough about Neil Riofski. He is a slender man with slack brown hair and dark doe's eyes. His laugh, a high-register hyena's bark, is rivaled in The Square as a shatterer of window panes only by Mary Etta's B-movie screech. Neil is a gentle soul, philosophical by nature. And there is a sadness to him. It is there in those dark eyes, the sadness perhaps of a man living with lost dreams, remembered ambitions.

"I've always been a night man," he says, banging away at the register. "In the day, I like my golf and my ponies. Ask Tommy here about the ponies." He pours a drink for Specs. "You know, the nature of this beast changes at night. In the day here, you get the real dynamics. That's when the biggies come in, attractive people, good mixers. The idea then is to get the customers to hang on long enough until Dennis can get to them with chitchat and keep them around for at least another round of CBAs. At night, you get the locals, the North Beach color. We even used to get some old Beats in here. I can remember when Gregory Corso used to come in all the time."

Bob Frugoli moves down from his end of the bar. "Neil, were you here the other day when Bruce Crow (another bartender) says to Moose, 'Ed, I just want to thank you for signing that union contract.'" Neil throws his hands up in horror. His laugh fills the room. "Yeah, well you can imagine. Ed just looks at him for a minute and then he says, 'You wanna thank me, huh. Well, here's what you're thanking me for: We're gonna have to sell this place because of that contract and when we do, you're gonna lose your job. You wanna thank me for that, go ahead.' So Bruce just kinda slinks away, and he comes up to me and says, 'You know, maybe I really don't belong here.' I just said, 'Bruce, I don't think I woulda said that one.'"

The Square's bartenders were almost silent witnesses to the tense struggle between their boss and the union activists in the waiters' corps. Their sympathies, however, were largely with management. To them, keeping The Square open was more important than winning a new contract. Besides, most of them, although long-term union members, have become cynical and disillusioned over the years with their benefits. "I told Herb Caen one day that if he's looking for real poverty-level people," Frugoli tells Neil, "he should find a retired bartender. That guy, I guarantee you, ain't getting shit." But Frugoli says he would not have crossed a picket line if one had been set up around his beloved place of business. And yet, of all his employees, Moose is closest to his bartenders. He sees them as kin, as macho guys, more macho, he suspects, than he will ever be. The waiters and waitresses seem to him more like smart-ass college kids always stirring up controversy. The bartenders (Crow now probably excepted) are the backbone of the joint. And they, for their part, do not see him as any sort of father figure. He's just the boss, and maybe on one of his good days, one of the boys. A strange boy, but still, at heart, one of them.

"I've been watching that man for ten years now," says Neil of Moose, "and I've yet to fathom his magic. You just can't get a handle on him. You watch him on point and he's brilliant. He keeps the biggies happy. He creates the aura of this place. He has such great recall of anything he's read that he can talk with the writers in here about their work. And he enjoys that repartee. No question, he knows how to pack this room." Neil snubs out a cigarette and riffles through some more of the night's receipts. "The dark side, of course, is the intensity. He's such a fiercely competitive man, a driven man. And he's impossible on the softball field." The laugh explodes. "At one of our Labor Day picnics, the staff got up a team to play Les Lapins. We called ourselves, in keeping with the French theme, the Base Canards. Well, Moose didn't have his whole team there, just a skeleton crew, and we won the damn game. You can imagine his reaction. He was stomping around all over the place. Finally, he comes up to me and puts his face right into mine. He's so close he's standing on my foot. Then he says, snarling, 'Now, when do you want to play our real team?' Can you believe that one? There's no way, of course, I want another game. What if we won again? I don't know how you figure a guy like that. He takes that softball *soooo* seriously. But then again, how do you knock those trips the team makes?"

Specs has been listening quietly, fingering a Scotch. He is a short, sturdy man with, as one might expect, unusually thick glasses. He has the look of a North Beach intellectual, and his talk is wry, understated. "Neil, did you hear the story about that first trip . . . to Paris?" Neil just smiles. He's packing away the liquor for the night. "Anyway, it seems George Yee and . . . that lawyer . . . yeah, Jimmy Igoe, . . . were on their way to the track, Longchamps, but neither of them speaks French, and they can't remember the name of the track, so when they get into a cab they've got no way of telling the driver where they want to go. Now Yee, who probably has a big heat on, decides to pantomime the whole thing for the driver. So he leans forward like a jockey and begins to bang his hip as if he were whipping a horse. The driver smiles and nods to show he understands perfectly. '*Oui*, monsieur,' he says, winking at Yee. George is pretty proud of himself, and Igoe is complimenting him on his ingenuity, when the cab pulls up in front of this building on a side street. Yee and Igoe just look at him funny. The cabby smiles and pats himself on the ass and points to the doorway, where some broad comes out. Then it dawns on them. The cabby has taken them to a whorehouse where the specialty is S&M." Neil almost chokes on his laugh.

The talk switches to the first night-baseball game at Wrigley Field in Chicago, played just the week before. Frugoli speaks with the authority of one who has played in the old ballpark, for Les Lapins against the supposed Chicago media stars. "What a beautiful place," he says, "day or night." "I think what they gotta watch out for is bugs," says Specs. "The whole Midwest is full of bugs, and when those lights go on, the bugs'll find out about it and be there. That's why they had to put a dome up in Houston. When they had the old open-air ballpark there, there were more mosquitoes in the stands than people. Like to have eaten everybody alive. That's one thing about San Francisco, no mosquitoes. No mosquitoes, that is, except for the one who spends every night in my bedroom." "Not just your bedroom," says Neil. "He gets over to my place, too." Specs looks at his watch. It is approaching one in the morning. "Holy shit, I gotta get over and close my joint before they tear it apart." He waves and trots out the front door. Neil, right behind him, pulls the shade down on the door and turns the lock as Specs leaves. The Square is officially closed.

But Neil and Frugoli stay on. They pour themselves drinks and shake dice to see who gets the lion's share of the tip jar. Neil wins. They lean back against the bar and relax for a moment before bagging the night's receipts and putting them in the safe. It has been a busy night, and the two bartenders toast each other on a job well done.

Outside, a dense and soggy fog has eased its weight on the silent city. The poplars across the street look damp and heavy. Cabbies in search of one last fare patrol Columbus Avenue. The spires of Saints Peter and Paul are only black shadows on a field of gray. It is dark there in the mist of early morning except for the pale lights of the Washington Square Bar & Grill. Already Wally Souza is stirring. The place must be opened for another day. And, God willing, another after that.

Epilogue

Hal Thunes died of cancer in November 1988. His old partner in merriment, Tom Slater, went back to work at The Square shortly before this sad event and remained there for a few months until he finally opened his own place, Clark's Corner Bar & Grill, across town on Potrero Hill.

On December 12, 1988, Manuel Saucedo arrived at The Square as usual at half past two in the afternoon to work his shift as night chef. As he walked through the front door, a nine-piece mariachi band struck up "The Anniversary Song," then switched quickly into "Paloma," whose onomatopoetic lyrics "cu-cu-ru-cu-cu" Manuel croons nightly to his fellow kitchen workers. Mark and Dennis O'Connor poured champagne at the bar, above which, strung across the giant mirror, was a sign reading, "Viva Manuel." It was the shy Mexican's fifteenth anniversary at The Square. Ed grabbed the microphone at the piano.

"Manuel Saucedo has been here since the first day we opened fifteen years ago," he began. "Somehow we're all still here. The trouble is, Manuel, we need you to work tonight." Laughter. "No, that's not true. You're off for the day. Have a good time. And, Manuel . . . we love you."

The odd part of that last remark is that it is undoubtedly true, for with all of the strife and divisiveness of recent months, there is yet much love inside those smoky grape walls. It is the one quality that separates the great saloons from ordinary eating and drinking establishments. It is the very lifeblood of this unusual place, the Washington Square Bar & Grill.

As the New Year began, The Square was still for sale. A high-powered downtown real-estate outfit had been employed to that end, and in the furtherance of its quest for a buyer, the company produced a videotape extolling the joint's unique virtues. The hope now is that if The Square is in fact sold, it will be kept intact as a sort of . . . yes . . . institution. Of course, it can never be the same, certainly not without the brilliant, volcanic, sometimes exasperating figure of Edward Moose IV, who, foibles aside, must be considered one of the premier saloonkeepers of our time. Who else, I submit to you, could have got quite so much mileage out of a silly softball team?

It is entirely possible, to be sure, that before the new year is out, The Square, as we've come to appreciate it, will be only another memory. Too bad. Yes, but oh, what a sweet and abiding memory!